Indiana
Atlas & Gazetteer™

Table of Contents

Important Notices

DeLorme has made reasonable efforts to provide you with
accurate maps and related information, but we cannot exclude
the possibility of errors or omissions in sources or of changes in
actual conditions. DELORME MAKES NO WARRANTIES OF
ANY KIND, EITHER EXPRESS OR IMPLIED, INCLUDING
THE WARRANTIES OF MERCHANTABILITY AND FITNESS
FOR A PARTICULAR PURPOSE. DELORME SHALL NOT
BE LIABLE TO ANY PERSON UNDER ANY LEGAL OR
EQUITABLE THEORY FOR DAMAGES ARISING OUT OF
THE USE OF THIS PUBLICATION, INCLUDING, WITHOUT
LIMITATION, FOR DIRECT, CONSEQUENTIAL
OR INCIDENTAL DAMAGES.

Nothing in this publication implies the right to use private property.
There may be private inholdings within the boundaries of public
reservations. You should respect all landowner restrictions.

Some listings may be seasonal or may have admission fees.
Please be sure to confirm this information when making plans.

Safety Information
To avoid accidents, always pay attention to actual road, traffic and
weather conditions and do not attempt to read these maps while you
are operating a vehicle. Please consult local authorities for the most
current information on road and other travel-related conditions.

Do not use this publication for marine or aeronautical
navigation, as it does not depict navigation aids, depths,
obstacles, landing approaches and other information
necessary to performing these functions safely.

THIRD EDITION
Copyright © 2004 DeLorme. All rights reserved.
P.O. Box 298, Yarmouth, Maine 04096
(207) 846-7000 www.delorme.com

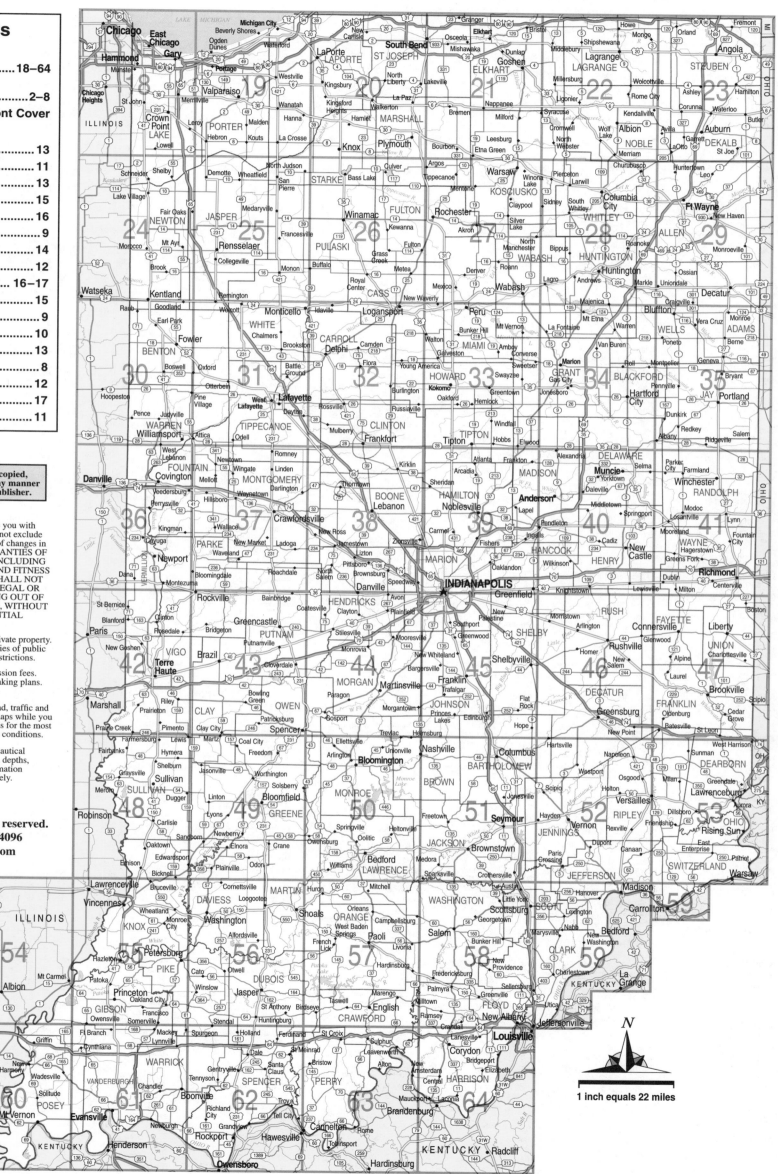

© DeLorme

N

1 inch equals 22 miles

Grid numbers refer to detailed map pages

W9-ATK-573

Index of Placenames and Map Features

ABOUT THE INDEX

This index contains over 5,300 features shown on the maps on pages 18–64. Names are listed alphabetically with map page(s) and grid coordinates to help locate them. The grid coordinates correspond to the letters (A–H) and numbers (1–12) along the top and outside edges of all map pages.

Guidelines for using this index:

- Placenames appear in boldface type, such as **Cedarville** 29 B9
- Drainage names (lakes, reservoirs, rivers, creeks, springs) appear in italic type, such as *Lake Pleasant* 23 A8
- Boundaried towns appear in capitals, such as FAYETTE 42 D4
- All other features (mountains, islands, points of interest, state and national lands, airports) appear in roman type, such as Shakamak State Park 49 B7
- Private campgrounds are listed with their corresponding four-digit numbers (used for locating on the maps) in parentheses, such as Hidden Lake Campground (4220) 33 G12
- Page number and grid coordinates are given for each occurrence of a name, such as *West Creek* 18 F4, H3; 24 A4

A

Aaron 53 G8
Aberdeen 53 F10
ABINGTON 41 H9; 47 A9
Abington 47 A10
Abner Creek 38 H4; 44 A4
ABOITE 28 D6
Aboite 28 E6
Aboite Creek 28 D6
Abydel 57 D9
Academie 29 B8
Ace Airpark 40 D2
Ackerman Ditch 26 F1
Acme 51 E9
Acton 45 B10
ADAMS 27 G7; 29 D9; 31 F7; 32 A2; 36 H6; 39 B7; 40 E2; 44 D2; 46 F3; 47 H8; 53 A8
Adams 44 E5; 46 G3
Adams Lake 22 D5
Adams Mill 32 E3
Adams Mill Bridge 32 E3
Adamsboro 26 H6
Add-More Campground (4000) 58 G6
ADDISON 45 D12
Ade 24 G4
Adel 49 B12
Advance 38 E2
Adventure Hiking Trail 63 B12
Adyeville 62 B6
Aetna 18 C6
Africa 62 G3
Agnew Ditch 26 E2
Aikman Creek 56 C3, D1
Ainsworth 18 E6
Aix 25 D8
Akron 27 D9
Alamo 37 E9
Alaska 44 E2
Albany 35 H7
ALBION 22 F4
Albion 22 F4; 59 A7
Aldine 26 B1
Aldrich Bend 60 D3
Alert 52 B1
Alexandria 34 H1; 40 A1
Alexandria Airport 40 A2
Alfont 39 F12
Alford 56 E1
Alfordsville 56 D4
Algiers 56 E1
Alida 19 E11
ALLEN 22 F6; 27 E8
Allen Branch of Hogan Creek 53 D9
Allen Crossing 52 C6
Allendale 42 F5
Allensville 53 G9
Alliance 40 D2
Allisonville 39 F9
Allman 44 C4
Alpine 47 D7
Alquina 47 C9
Alta 36 H5
Altamont Switch 31 G11
Alto 33 F8
Alton 63 C10
Altona 23 G8
Alvarado 23 D11
Ambia 30 E3
Amboy 33 C10
American Bottoms 49 D12
Americus 31 D12
Ames 37 D11
Amish Acres 21 F9
Amishville USA 35 C10
Amishville USA Campground (4010) 35 C10
Amity 45 F9
Amo 44 B2
ANDERSON 40 D1; 46 E4; 61 F12; 63 D7
Anderson 40 C1
Anderson Municipal Airport–Darlington Field 40 C2
Anderson River 62 B6, D6; 63 A7
Anderson University 40 C2
Anderson's Orchard & Winery 19 D10
Andersonville 40 A4; 46 E6
Andrews 28 G2
Andry 19 A12
Angel Mounds State Historic Site 61 F10
Angola 23 C10
Anita 45 F7
Annapolis 36 G6
Anoka 32 A6
Anthony 34 H4
Anthony Creek 40 H2
Antioch 35 G10; 38 A3
Antiville 35 E10
Antrim Ditch 25 C10, D11
Apalona 63 B8
Arba 41 E11
Arcadia 39 B9
Arcana 34 D3
Arcola 28 C6
Arda 55 D12
Ardmore 20 B6
Arens Field (airport) 26 C2
Aretz Airport 31 E11
Arganbright Hill 44 G2
Argos 27 A7
Arlington 46 B3; 50 B3
Armiesburg 42 A5
ARMSTRONG 61 C8
Armstrong 61 C8
Arney 49 A10
Arnold Creek 53 F11
Aroma 39 B11
Arrowhead Golf Course 40 G1
Arrowhead Park 21 H12
Art 43 F8
Arthur 56 G1
Artic 23 E12
Artist Point 63 B11
Ash Grove 31 D11
Ash Iron Springs 62 D1
Ashboro 43 F8
Asher Branch of Wabash River 33 A10
Asherville 43 E9
ASHLAND 44 E2
Ashland 40 F6
Ashley 23 D9
Asphaltum 25 C10
Athens 27 D8
Atherton 42 C5
Atkinson 31 D7
Atkinsonville 43 G11
Atlanta 39 A9
Atterbury Fish and Wildlife Area 45 G9
Attica 31 H7
Atwood 27 A10
Atwood Lake 22 D4
AUBBEENAUBBEE 26 C4
Auburn 23 G9
Auburn Junction 23 G9
Auburn–Cord–Duesenberg Museum 23 G9
Augusta 39 G7; 56 G1
Augusta Hills Golf Course 22 F4
Augusta Lake 56 G1
Aultshire 40 A5
Aurora 53 D11
Aurora Bend 42 H2
Austin 58 A6
Auten Ditch 20 C6
Avalon 29 E8
Avalon Hills 39 G9
Avery 32 H4
Avilla 23 G7
Avoca 50 F3
Avon 44 A5
Avonburg 53 G7
Aylesworth 37 B7
Ayrshire 56 G1
Azalia 51 C11

B

Babcock 19 D8
Bachelor Creek 27 G10
Bachelor Run 32 C3, E4
Back Creek 34 F2; 50 F6, H6
Backcountry Loop 58 A3
Bacon 57 F10
Bacon Prairie Creek 39 A10
Badger Creek 34 B1
Badger Grove 31 C10
Baerfield 29 E7
Bailey Ditch 20 G1; 24 A4
Baileys Corner 25 D10
Bailly/Chellberg Trail 19 C8
BAINBRIDGE 56 F4
Bainbridge 43 A12
Bainter Town 21 D12
BAKER 44 G2; 50 G1
BAKER 48 C6; 49 G12
Baker Hill 50 A6
Bakers Camp Bridge 43 A12
Bakers Corner 39 C8
Bakerstown 22 G5
Balbec 35 D8
Bald Hill 43 C10; 55 G9
Bald Knob 58 G6
Bald Knobs 51 D7
Baldridge 48 A5
Ball Lake 23 D10
Ball State University 40 B4
Ballstown 53 A7
Baltzell–Lenhart Woods Nature Preserve 29 H10
Bandmill 55 D8
Bandon 63 C8
Banning Corner 31 G8
Banquo 34 B2
Banta 45 D7
Bar-Barry Heights 31 E11
Barbee 22 H1
Barbersville 52 F6
Barce 30 C6
Bargersville 45 D7
BARKLEY 25 D8
Barnard 38 G1
Barnard Hill 44 E5
Barnes Creek 45 G7
Barnes–Seng Wetland Conservation Area 56 G4
Barnhart Town 42 E4
BARR 56 B3
Barr Creek 61 C7
Barr Lake 27 C8
Barren Creek 34 F2
Barren Fork of Little Pigeon Creek 62 B1, C1
Barrett 60 B5
Barrick Corner 49 A9
Barten Ditch 24 G6
Bartle 58 D5
Bartlettsville 50 E4
BARTON 55 H10; 61 A10
Bartonia 41 C11
Bascom Corner 53 F10
Bass 26 B2
Bass Lake 26 A2
Bass Lake 26 A2
Bass Lake State Beach 26 A3
Bates Ridge 52 F6
Batesville 47 H7
BATH 47 E11
Bath 47 E11
Battle Ground 31 E11
Baugh City 61 D11
Baughman Hill 50 A6
BAUGO 21 B9
Baugo Creek 21 B9, D9
Bayfield 22 H1
Beach Creek 49 B10
Beal 55 D8
Beal Taylor Ditch 28 D5
Beamer 43 G10
BEAN BLOSSOM 44 H2; 50 A2
Bean Blossom Bridge 50 A6
Beanblossom 45 H7
Beanblossom Creek 44 H2, H4; 50 A3, A4, A6
Bear Branch 53 F9
Bear Branch of Bear Creek 53 F8
BEAR CREEK 35 D10
Bear Creek 35 D10, E10, H9; 39 B11; 41 A9, G7; 52 B1, C1, C3, G2; 53 F8; 56 E2; 58 F3; 63 F9
Bear Hill 49 H12
Bear Lake 22 H3
Beard 32 G4
Beardstown 26 C2
Beargrass Creek 27 F12; 28 F1
Bearwallow Hill 51 A7
Beason Ditch 35 G9
Beatrice 19 F7
Beatty Walker Ditch 51 F9
Beattys Corner 19 C11
BEAVER 24 E4; 25 F12; 26 E1
Beaver City 24 F5
Beaver Creek 24 E4; 35 D7; 57 A8, B7
Beaver Dam 27 C9
Beaver Dam Lake 27 C9; 56 F5
Beaver Lake Ditch 24 C4, D5
Beaver Meadow Creek 46 B2
Beaver Ridge Family Camping (4020) 20 D6
Beaverdam Creek 60 G4
Bebout Creek 46 C3
Becks Grove 51 C8
Becks Mill 58 D2
Beckville 38 E1
Bedford 50 G4
Bee Ridge 43 D7
BEECH CREEK 49 C12; 50 C1
Beech Creek 49 D12; 50 D1
Beech Grove 45 A8
Beech Hills 55 D11
Beechwood 63 A10
Beechwood Golf Course 20 C1
Beehunter 49 E8
Beehunter Ditch 49 D8
Beeson Bridge 37 H7; 43 A7
Beesons 47 A8
Behlmer Corner 53 B7
Belknap 61 E7
Bell Center 26 G2
Bell Creek 40 B4, C4, E4
Bell Ditch 31 B10
Bell Rohr Park 21 G12
Belle Union 44 D1
Belleview 52 G5
Belleville 44 B4
Bellfountain 35 F11
Bellmore 43 A8
Bells Ford Bridge 51 E10
Belmont 50 B5
Belshaw 24 A4
Ben Davis 44 A6
Ben Davis Creek 46 C5
Ben Hur Museum 37 D11
Benefiel Corner 48 C5
Bengal 45 E10
Benham 53 E7
Bennetts Switch 33 C8
Bennettsville 58 F6
Bennington 53 G8
BENTON 21 E12; 44 H4; 50 A4
Benton 21 E12
Bentonville 47 A7
Benwood 43 D8
Berlein 23 C11
Berlin Court Ditch 21 F10
Berne 35 B10
Berns–Meyer Nature Preserve 26 E2
Berry Ridge 51 D7
Best Ditch 24 B3
Bethany 44 D5
BETHEL 60 A4
Bethel 40 A3; 41 E12
Bethel College 21 B7
Bethel Village 51 B10
BETHLEHEM 26 G6; 59 D9
Bethlehem 59 D10
Beverly Hill 19 D10
Beverly Shores 19 B10
Bice Ditch 25 G8
Bicknell 48 H6
Big Barbee Lake 22 H1
Big Bayou 60 A5, B4
Big Blue River 40 E5, G4, H3; 45 C12, D12, E11, G10; 46 A3, B1
Big Bottom 56 G3
Big Branch Creek 48 C6
Big Cedar Creek 47 E11, F11
Big Chapman Lake 21 H12
Big Chapman Lake Nature Preserve 21 H12
Big Clifty Creek 52 H4
BIG CREEK 31 B11
Big Creek 31 B9, B12; 52 E5, G4, H2, H3; 60 C6, D5, E3; 61 B8, B10, B11, B12
Big Ditney Hill 61 C11
Big Duck Creek 33 H12
Big Eagle Creek 38 F6
Big Hog Creek 59 B7
Big Hurricane Hill 44 E3
Big Indian Creek 28 D5
Big Lake 22 H3
Big Lick Creek 34 F6, G4
Big Long Lake 23 D7
Big Monon Creek 25 G12
Big Monon Ditch 25 B12, D12, E11, F12
Big Ox Creek 58 A6, C6
Big Pine Creek 30 F6, G6, H6; 31 C7, C8, E7
Big Pine Creek Ditch 31 B7
Big Raccoon Creek 37 F12, G11, H10; 38 E2; 42 B6
Big Rocky Fork Bridge 43 B9
Big Run 23 F12
Big Shawnee Creek 36 A6; 37 A8
Big Spring Nature Preserve 58 E2
Big Springs 38 D6
Big Springs 59 A9
Big Turkey Lake 23 C7
Big Walnut Creek 37 H12; 38 H1; 43 A12, B11, D10
BIGGER 52 E4
Billie Creek Bridge 43 A7
Billie Creek Village 43 A7
Billingsville 47 D11
Billtown 43 E7
Billville 43 E8
Binkley Hill 64 B2
Bippus 28 F2
Birch Creek 43 E8, G8; 56 E3
Birchim 20 A2
Birdseye 57 H7
Birmingham 27 F8
Bischoff Reservoir 47 H7
BLACK 60 F4
Black Ankle Creek 49 F12
Black Creek 23 H7; 34 B4; 37 D10; 49 D7, E8, G7; 53 F7
Black Oak 18 D5; 56 B3
Black River 60 A6, B5; 61 A7
Black Rock 31 G8
Black Squirrel Golf Club 21 D11
Blackhawk 42 H6
Blackhawk Beach 19 D9
Blackhawk Campground (4030) 43 E11
Blackman Lake 22 D6
Blackthorn Golf Club 20 A6
Blaine 35 F9
Blairsville 60 D6
Blanford 42 B3
Blocher 59 A8
Bloomer 39 C12
BLOOMFIELD 22 B4
Bloomfield 49 D10; 62 D2
Bloomfield Barrens Nature Preserve 62 D2
BLOOMING GROVE 47 E8
Blooming Grove 47 E9
Bloomingdale 37 G7
Bloomingport 41 D10
BLOOMINGTON 50 A3
Bloomington 50 B3
Blountsville 41 D7
Blue 53 F9
Blue Babe Branch of Blue River 28 A3
Blue Chip Casino 19 A11
BLUE CREEK 35 A11
Blue Creek 35 A9, A12, B11; 47 G9, H9; 56 D6
Blue Lake 28 A5
Blue Lick 58 E6
Blue Ridge 46 D2
BLUE RIVER 40 E6, H1; 45 F9; 46 A1; 58 G1
Blue River 58 D4
Blue River 22 H5; 28 A5, C4; 57 G12, H12; 58 D2, F1; 63 A12
Blue Spring Hollow 63 C12
Bluecast 29 B11
Bluecast Spring 29 B11
Bluespring Caverns 50 H3
Bluff Creek 45 D7
Bluff Point 35 G10
Bluffs 44 D6
Bluffton 35 A7
Blunk Point 64 C4
Bobtown 51 D10
BOGARD 49 H8; 56 A3
Bogard Creek 49 F11; 57 H10
Boggs Creek 49 H11; 56 B5
Boggstown 45 D11
Bogle Corner 49 B7
Bogus Run 19 H12; 25 A12; 26 A1, B1
Bohnke Ditch 29 E11
BOLIVAR 31 D7
Bolivar 27 E12
Bolley Ditch 27 E10
Bonds 57 B8
Bonneyville Mill 21 A12
BONO 57 A11
Bono 42 A4; 57 A12
BOON 61 D12; 62 D1
BOONE 19 H8; 26 G3; 33 G12; 34 G1; 56 E3; 63 B10; 64 D3
Boone Cave 50 A1
Boone County Airport 38 E4
Boone Grove 19 G8
Boonville 61 D12
Boonville Airport 61 D12
Boot Lake 21 A9
Border Ditch 21 G8
Borns Winery 59 A11
Borum Run 29 H10
BOSTON 47 A11
Boston 47 A11
Boston Corner 29 F11
Boswell 30 D5
Boundary City 35 G10
Boundary Hill 47 F9
BOURBON 21 G8
Bourbon 21 H8
Bower Creek 37 B12
Bowers 38 B1
Bowerstown 28 G4
Bowery Creek 58 E6
Bowling Green 43 G9
Bowman 55 E11
Bowsher Ford Bridge 36 F5
Boxley 39 B7
Boyd 46 A3
Boyd Branch of Laughery Creek 53 D8
Boyd Hill 63 E7
Boyleston 32 H5
Bracht Ditch 29 H9
Bracken 28 E2
Bradfield Corner 42 A6
Bradford 58 G3
Bradley Ridge 50 B6
Bramble 49 H11
Branchville 63 B9
BRANDYWINE 45 A12, D11
Brandywine Creek 40 G1; 45 A12, C12
Braxtons Siding 57 D10
Braysville 47 H11
Braytown 59 G11
BRAZIL 43 D8
Brazil 43 D8
Brazil–Clay County Airport 43 E8
Breckenridge 64 A3
Breezy Point 31 B12
Bremen 21 F8
Brems 20 G1
Brendonwood 39 G9
Bretzville 56 H5
Brewer Ditch 49 E7
Brewer Hill 49 F9
Brewersville 52 C2
Brewery Hill 60 E4
Breyfogel Ditch 19 H7
Briar Leaf Golf Club 20 B1
Briarwood 44 D3
Brice 35 F11
Brick Chapel 43 A11
Brickyard Crossing Golf Course 39 H7
Bridge Creek 32 D1; 49 D12
Bridgeport 44 A6; 64 B5
Bridgeton 43 B7
Bridgeton Bridge 43 B7
Briggs 28 C4
Bright 53 A11
Brighton 22 A6
Brimfield 22 E5
Brinckley 41 A8
Bringhurst 32 D3
Brisco 30 F5
Bristol 21 A12
Bristow 63 C7
Britton Golf Course 39 E9
Britton Hill 58 G1
Broad Park 44 C1
Broad Pond 54 G6
Broad Ripple 39 G8
Broadmoor 39 G7
Broadview 50 C3
Brock Creek 58 C2
Brock Ridge 64 A4
Brock–Sampson Nature Preserve 64 A5
Bromer 57 C11
Brook 24 G5
Brook Hill Golf Club 47 F9
Brookfield 45 C10
Brookhaven 34 D2
Brooklyn 44 D5
Brookmoor 44 D5
Brooks Creek 35 E8, G9
Brooksburg 59 G10
Brookside Estates 29 B9
Brookston 31 C11
BROOKVILLE 47 F10
Brookville 47 F9
Brookville Lake 47 D9
Brookville Lake Project 47 E10, F10
Broom Hill 58 F5
Brouillettes Creek 42 B3
BROWN 37 F9; 38 F5; 40 F1; 44 C5; 53 E7; 57 B12
BROWN 49 H11
Brown County State Park 51 B7
Brown County Winery 51 A7
Brown Ditch 24 A5; 25 F11; 55 F7, G8
Brown Hill 51 A7
Brown Jug Corner 42 H6
Brown Ridge 50 B5
Browning Hill 50 D6
Browns Crossing 44 F3
Browns Valley 37 F10
Browns Wonder Creek 38 B4
Brownsburg 38 G5
BROWNSTOWN 51 F8
Brownstown 51 G9; 57 G9
BROWNSVILLE 47 B9
Brownsville 47 B9
Bruce Ditch 24 A4
Bruce Lake 26 D5
Bruce Lake 26 C4
Bruce Lake Outlet 26 C4
Bruceville 55 A11
Brummetts Creek 50 B5
Brunerstown 43 B10
Brunner Hill 58 G2
Brunswick 18 G3; 49 B8
Brush Creek 38 B3; 43 G8; 49 B10; 51 B11; 52 C4
Brush Creek Fish and Wildlife Area 52 D3
Brush Creek Reservoir 52 D3
Brush Fork of Tanners Creek 53 A11
Brush Heap Creek 64 A2
Brushy Fork of Indian Kentuck Creek 53 H7
Brushy Prairie 23 B7
Bryan Nature Preserve 32 G2
Bryant 35 D10
Bryant Creek 44 G3
Bryant Ditch 18 H6
Bryantsburg 52 G5
Bryantsville 50 H3
Buchanan 64 A5
Buchanan Corner 49 B7
BUCK CREEK 39 H11
Buck Creek 31 E12
Buck Creek 22 B3; 31 E12; 33 H9; 36 H4; 39 G11, H10; 40 B4, C5, H3, H5; 45 A10, B10; 48 C4, D5; 49 D8; 64 B4, C2, D2
Buck Creek Ditch 32 E1
Buck Knob 56 A6
Buckeye 34 B5
Buckhart Creek 45 F9
Buckskin 61 A11
Bucktown 48 E6
Bud 45 H7
Budd Fisher Ditch 26 E1
Buddha 50 H5
Buena Vista 41 C9; 46 F6; 55 E10; 64 D4
Buffalo 26 G1
Buffalo Creek 58 A1
Buffalo Flat 56 F5
Buffaloville 62 C4
Buffington Harbor 18 B4
Bufkin 60 E5
Bull Creek 28 F5
Bull Fork of Salt Creek 46 E6
Bull Rapids 29 B11
Bull Run 18 F4
Bullocktown 62 E1
Bulls Point 63 C11
Bunch Ditch of East Branch of Stock Ditch 21 E7
Bunch Ditch of West Branch of Stock Ditch 21 E7
Bunker Hill 33 B8; 44 D4; 47 C7; 58 D5
Burdick 19 C10
Burgett Ditch 26 G2
Burket 27 B10
Burkhart Creek 44 F3
BURLINGTON 32 E4
Burlington 32 E5
Burlington Beach 19 E9
Burnett 42 D6
Burnett Creek 31 D10, D11, E11
Burnetts Creek 32 A2
Burnettsville 32 A2
Burney 46 H2
Burns City 49 H11
Burns Harbor 19 C8
Burnsville 52 B1
Burr Creek 27 H12; 28 H1
Burr Lake 26 A5
Burr Oak 22 H4
Burrows 32 B3
Busching Bridge 53 D7
Bush Creek 41 A8
Bushrod 49 E8
BUSSERON 48 G3
Busseron 48 G4
Busseron Creek 48 A6, B6, D5, F4
BUTLER 23 H8; 33 B9; 47 G8
Butler 23 F11
Butler Center 23 H8
Butler Creek 44 F2
Butler Falls 59 B10
Butler University 39 G7
Butler Winery 50 B3
Butlers Creek 47 A9
Butlerville 52 D3
Buttermilk Creek 48 D5
Butternut Creek 35 G9
Butternut Springs 19 D8
Buzzard Hollow 57 D8
Buzzard Roost Hill 57 H12
Byrneville 58 H3
Byron 20 B2; 37 F8

C

Cabin Creek 41 C8
Caborn 60 E6
Cades Mill Bridge 36 D6
Cadiz 40 F4
Cady Marsh Ditch 18 D5
CAESAR CREEK 53 E8
Caesar Creek 53 D8
Cagles Mill 43 E10
Cagles Mill Lake 43 E10
Cagles Mill Lake Project 43 E11
CAIN 37 C8
Cairo 31 D10
Caldwell Lake 27 C10
Cale 49 H12
Caledonia 48 C5
CALIFORNIA 26 A1
Callahan Ditch 25 D9
CALUMET 18 C5
Calumet Harbor 18 A3
Calvertville 49 C11
Cambria 32 G3
Cambridge City 41 H7
Camby 44 B6
Camden 32 C3
Cammack 40 A4
Camp Atterbury Maneuver Training Center 45 G9, H9; 51 A9
Camp Brosend 61 E11
Camp Creek 59 D10
Camp Flat Rock 46 F1
Camp Fork Creek 57 G10
Camp Roberts 51 B7
Camp Run 35 D9
Camp Shor 53 E11
CAMPBELL 52 D3; 61 D10
Campbell Corner 48 B5
Campbell Creek 40 A6; 41 A7
Campbell Ditch 35 D9
Campbells Run 32 F2, F3
Campbellsburg 57 B12
Campbelltown 56 F1
Canaan 52 G6
Candleglo Village 45 D12
Candy Stripe Campsite (4040) 19 F8
Cane Creek South 57 E7
Cane Green Bottom 49 F7
Caney Creek 62 E1, H2
Cannelburg 56 B4
Cannelton 63 F7
Cannelton Locks and Dam Project 63 F8
Cantaloupe 55 D9
Canton 58 C3
Cape Sandy 63 B11
Capehart 56 A1
Carbon 43 C8
Carbondale 30 G5
Cardonia 43 D8
Carefree 63 A11
Carlisle 48 E5
Carlos 41 D9
Carmel 39 E8
Carnahan Ditch No 2 26 G1
Carp 43 G12
CARPENTER 25 H7; 31 A7
Carpenter Creek 25 F7, H7; 31 A7
Carpentersville 37 H12
CARR 51 H7; 58 F5
Carr Lake 27 B11
Carrolls 29 B8
CARROLLTON 32 D4
Carrollton 32 D5; 45 A12
Cart Creek 33 B12; 34 C1
CARTER 62 B4
Carters Creek 57 C11
Cartersburg 44 B4
Carthage 46 A3
Carwood 58 F5
Cary 43 A12
Cascade 50 B3
CASS 19 F11; 25 C11; 26 G2; 43 F9; 48 C6; 49 F9; 53 F9; 56 H3; 62 A3
Cass 48 C6
Cass Lake 22 B2
Cassville 33 D8
Castle Garden 61 D11
Castleton 39 F9
Cataract 43 F12
Cataract Falls Bridge 43 F12
Cates 36 E5
Catherine Creek 51 A9
Catlin 43 B7
Catlin Bridge 37 H7
Cato 56 F1
Cave Spring 57 F12
Cayuga 36 F4
Cecil M Harden Lake 37 H9; 43 A9
Cecil M Harden Lake Project 43 A9
Cedar 23 H8
Cedar Canyons 29 A8
Cedar Chapel Bridge 39 E9
CEDAR CREEK 24 A5; 29 A9
Cedar Creek 18 H5; 23 E9, G9, H8; 24 A4; 29 A8, A9
Cedar Grove 47 G10
Cedar Lake 18 G4
Cedar Lake 18 G4; 23 E9; 28 A4
Cedar Lake Branch of Elder Ditch 28 A2
Cedar Lake Golf Course 22 A5
Cedar Lake Monastery Golf Club 18 G4
Cedar Point 26 A2
Cedar Shores 29 A9
Cedar Swamp Wetland Conservation Area 23 A11
Cedarville 29 B9
Cedarville Reservoir 29 A9
Celestine 56 G6
Celina 63 B8
Celina Lake 63 B8
Cementville 59 G7
Centenary 42 B4
Centennial 37 E7

continue on next page

continue on next page

Roselawn 24 B6
Roseville Bridge 42 B6
Rosewood 64 D4
ROSS 18 E6; 32 G2
Ross 18 D5
Ross Run 27 H12; 28 H1
Rossburg 46 H6
Rosston 38 D6
Rosstown 51 C10
Rossville 32 F2
Roth Park 32 B1
Round Barn Theater 21 F9
ROUND GROVE 31 C9
Round Grove 31 C9
Round Hill 53 B9
Round Knob 58 D5
Round Lake 23 E7; 27 E11; 28 A4
Round Lake Wetland Conservation Area and Nature Preserve 26 A2
Rowe Eden Ditch 22 C2
Royal Center 26 G4
Royal Oaks 29 C9
Royalton 38 F5
Royer Lake (Sloan Lake) 22 C5
Royerton 40 A5
Royville 29 B8
Rozella Ford Golf Club 27 A11
Rugby 46 H1
Runnymede 19 H11
Runyantown 59 E8
Rupert's Resort Campground (4530) 21 F7
Rural 41 C10
Rush Creek 34 A2; 36 G6; 58 B1; 60 D5
Rush Creek Bridge 36 F6
Rush Creek Valley 58 B1
Rush Ridge 50 C4
RUSHVILLE 46 C4
Rushville 46 C4
Rusk 56 D6
RUSSELL 37 H10
Russell Lake 38 F6
Russellville 37 G10
Russiaville 32 F6
Rustic Hills 61 E11
RUTHERFORD 56 D5
Ruthmere Museum 21 B10
Rutland 26 A5
Ryan Ditch 25 C10, D9, E9

S

S & H Campground (4540) 39 H11
Salamonia 35 G11
SALAMONIE 34 B4
Salamonie Lake 28 H2; 34 A2
Salamonie Lake Project 28 H1, H2; 34 A2, A3
Salamonie River 28 H1; 34 A3, C5; 35 D7, F9, F11
SALEM 23 D8; 25 E11; 40 C3
Salem 35 A11, H11; 47 C11; 58 C2
Salem Center 23 C8
Salem Heights 20 D2
Salem Municipal Airport 58 C2
Salem Ridge 53 E11
Saline City 43 G8
Sally Doty Hill 45 D7
Sally Hill 57 A9
SALT CREEK 46 H5; 47 F7; 50 C4; 51 E7
Salt Creek 19 D8, F9; 41 B10; 46 G5, G6; 47 F7; 50 E3, F3, G3
Salt Creek Golf Club 51 B7
Salt Fork of Tanners Creek 53 A11
Saltillo 57 B12
SALUDA 59 C9
Saluda 59 B10
Samaria 45 F7
Sampson Hill 56 C6
San Jacinto 52 E4
San Pierre 25 B11
SAND CREEK 46 H3; 51 C11; 52 A2, C2
Sand Creek 19 C9; 39 E10; 46 G4, H3; 51 D12; 52 A3, B3, D1; 55 H10
Sand Hill 23 E7; 43 F11; 49 F11; 55 G8; 64 C1
Sand Lake 22 G5
Sand Lick Creek 43 H11
Sand Ridge 62 F1
Sand Ridge Trail 26 C2
Sandborn 49 F7
Sandcut 42 D6
Sanders 50 C3
Sandford 42 D3
Sandhill Nature Preserve 26 B2
Sandusky 46 F4
Sandy Beach 31 B12
Sandy Creek 62 E4
Sandy Hook 56 D1
Sandy Hook Ditch 19 H8
Sandytown 42 B4
Sanes Creek 46 D6; 47 E7
Santa Claus 62 C5
Santa Fe 33 B10
Saratoga 41 A11
Sardinia 52 B3
Sassafras 63 B7
Satan Hill 43 G10
Saturn 28 D5
Saugany Lake 20 A3
Savah 60 D4
Sawdon Ridge 53 A11
Scalesville 62 A1
Scarce of Fat Ridge 50 A5
Scarlet 57 B7
Scenic Campground (4550) 47 F10
Scenic Hill 56 B5
Scenic Hills Campground (4560) 22 A1
Schaefer Lake 45 H12; 46 H1
Schatzley Ditch 25 A8
Schererville 18 E4
Scherwood Golf 18 E4
Schley 62 D5
Schneider 24 B4
Schnellville 56 G6
Scholtz Ditch 25 B11, C12
School Branch of Big Eagle Creek 38 G5
Schoolhouse Hill 56 C6; 58 G1
Science Central 29 C8
SCIPIO 19 D12; 20 D1; 29 A11
Scipio 47 F12; 52 C1
Scipio Bridge 52 C1
Scircleville 32 H6
Scotchtown 48 D6
Scotland 49 F11
SCOTT 21 F9; 23 B10; 37 F11; 61 C9
Scott 22 A3
Scott City 48 B4
Scott Corner 41 C8
Scott Ditch 54 H6
Scott Hill 63 A12
Scotts Ridge 53 G7
Scottsburg 58 B6
Scottsburg Airport 58 B6
Scottsburg Reservoir 58 B6
Scottsville 58 F5
Scudder Hill 48 H6
Scuffle Creek 35 C7
Seafield 31 A10
Searcy Crossroads 53 G11
Sechrist Lake 22 H1
Sedalia 32 F3
Sedan 23 F8
Sedley 19 E8
Seed Tick Creek 56 A5
Seegar Ditch 28 C6
Seelyville 42 E6
Sefert Hill 56 B2
Seigs Hill 58 H1
Sellersburg 58 F6
Selma 40 B6
Selmier State Forest 52 D2
Selvin 62 A2
Servel Lake 61 F7
Servia 28 E1
Seton Knob 57 H10
Sevastopol 27 C9
Seven Springs 64 B4
Sevenmile Bend 55 E11
SEWARD 27 C10
Sexson Spring 50 F1
Sexton 46 B4
Seyberts 22 A3
Seymour 51 E11
Seymour Elks Golf Club 51 F10
Shadeland 31 G10; 34 C2
Shades State Park 37 F8, F9
Shades State Park Airport 37 F9
Shades State Park Trails 37 F9
Shadowood Golf Course 51 E11
Shady Banks 21 F12
Shady Lane 43 D9
Shady Lawn 18 F5
Shady Nook 23 D7
Shakamak State Park 49 B7
Shaker Run 47 A7
Shamrock Lake 34 F4
Shanghai 32 F6
Shankatank Creek 46 A5
Shannondale 38 D1
Shanty Falls 27 H11
Sharon 32 D5
Sharpsville 33 G8
Sharptown 47 G11
Shaw Loop 58 C6
SHAWNEE 36 A6
Shawnee Creek 46 A6
Shawnee Field (airport) 49 D9
SHAWSWICK 50 G4
Shawswick 50 F5
Sheets Ditch 26 H4
Sheff 30 A4
SHEFFIELD 31 H12; 32 G1
Shelburn 48 B5
SHELBY 31 E9; 45 E12; 46 E1; 52 E5, G6
Shelby 24 B5
Shelbyville 45 D12
Shelbyville Municipal Airport 45 D12
Sheldon Arm 19 E12
Sheldon Swope Art Museum 42 E5
Shenk Airport 23 H7
Shepard Hill 51 C7
Shepardsville 42 C4
Shepherd 38 E4
Sheridan 39 C7
Sheridan Airport 39 B7
Shideler 34 H5
Shields 51 F9
Shieldstown Bridge 51 F9
Shiloh 48 D6
Shipshewana 22 B3
Shipshewana Campground & Amish Log Cabin Lodging (4580) 22 A2
Shipshewana Campground (4570) 22 B3
Shipshewana Lake 22 B2
Shireman Hill 64 D1
Shirley 40 F3
Shoals 56 B6
Shooters Hill 39 G7
Shore Acres 39 G8
Short Creek 56 H4; 62 A4
Shrader–Weaver Nature Preserve 47 A7
Shrader–Weaver Woods 47 A7
Shriner Lake 28 A4
Shumaker Ridge 44 D2
Siberia 63 A7
Sidney 28 C1
Sidney Branch of Flatrock River 45 G12
Sigler Creek 63 A7
Silex 44 G2
SILVER CREEK 58 G6
Silver Creek 27 D10, E11; 28 F2; 47 A11, B10; 58 E6, G6; 59 D7, G7
Silver Lake 27 D11
Silver Lake 20 B2; 23 C9; 27 C11
Silverdale 62 F3
Silverville 50 G2
Silverwood 36 E5
Sim Smith Bridge 36 H6
Simison Creek 35 G12
Simonton Creek 28 E1
Simonton Lake 21 A10
Simonton Lake 21 A10
Simpson 28 G5
Simpson Corner 37 B7
Simpson Creek 47 B9
Simpson Hill 49 E9
SIMS 33 D11
Sims 33 E11
Singer Ditch 49 F7
Singleton Ditch 24 A5
Sinking Fork of Silver Creek 59 E7
Sipe Ditch 35 F9
Sisson 55 D9
Sitka 26 H1
Six Mile Creek 40 G2, H2; 46 A2
Six Points 43 G10; 44 A5
Sixmile Creek 35 B8, C8; 43 G9; 52 D1, F1
SKELTON 62 C1
Skelton 56 G4
Skinner Lake 22 F5
Sky King Airport 42 D5
Skylane Airport 61 D8
Slash Creek 45 F11
Slate Creek 56 E4
Sleepy Hollow 47 F11
Sleeth 32 B1
Slider Cave 59 A9
Sloan 30 H4
Sloan Branch of Clifty Creek 51 A11
Sloan Ditch 49 C9
Slocum Ditch 19 F11
Slough Creek 25 F7, F9
Sly Fork of Fall Creek 40 D2
Smalley Lake 22 H3
Smalls Creek 45 H5; 55 A10
Smart Ditch 51 H10
Smartsburg 37 D12
Smedley 58 C1
SMITH 28 A5; 49 C8; 61 B7
Smith 20 A1
Smith Bridge 46 C5
Smith Creek 47 A10
Smith Field (airport) 29 B8
Smith Fork of Pigeon Creek 61 A10, A12
Smith Hill 58 D1
Smith Valley 45 C7
SMITHFIELD 23 E9
Smithfield 40 B6
Smithland 45 E11; 46 H5
Smiths Crossing 46 H5
Smithson 31 A11
Smithville 43 H9; 50 D3
Smock Golf Course 45 C8
Smockville 43 C8
Smoke Corner 19 F9
Smoky Hollow 50 C5
Smothers Creek 49 H7, H9; 56 A1
SMYRNA 52 H3
Smyrna 52 A5, H4
Smythe 61 E10
Snacks 38 G6
Snail Creek 45 C11
Snake Creek 43 C10; 44 D3
Snake Run 61 A10
Snow Ditch 31 A12
Snow Hill 41 C10
Snow Hill 47 G11
Snow Hill Bridge 47 H11
Snyder Hill 43 D11
Solitude 60 E5
Solon Ditch 28 B5
Solsberry 49 C12
Somerset 33 B12
Somerville 55 H11
South Bend 21 B7
South Bend East KOA (4590) 21 A8
South Bethany 51 B9
South Boston 58 C4
South Branch of Clifty Creek 46 F4
South Branch of Elkhart River 22 F3
South Branch of Garrison Creek 47 D7
South Branch of Hursey Ditch 23 H10
South Center 20 E2
South Chain Lake 20 B5
South Clear Lake 20 A5
South Elwood 39 A11
South Fork of Beaver Creek 57 B7
South Fork of Blue River 58 D5, E3, F2
South Fork of Buck Creek 64 C4
South Fork of Deer Creek 33 C7, D8
South Fork of Laughery Creek 53 E9, F9
South Fork of Leatherwood Creek 50 G5
South Fork of Little Raccoon Creek 37 H9
South Fork of Little Salt Creek 46 E6
South Fork of Lost River 57 C12
South Fork of Pakota River 55 G12; 56 H1
South Fork of Prairie Creek 56 A2
South Fork of Salt Creek 50 D6; 51 E7
South Fork of White Creek 51 D9
South Fork of Wildcat Creek 31 F12, G12; 32 G1, H2, H5
South Gate 47 H10
South Gleason Golf Course 18 D5
South Grove Golf Course 39 H7
South Harrison Lake 51 B9
South Haven 19 D8; 27 H11
South Hogan Creek 53 C7, D8, D9
South LaPorte 20 D1
South Marion 25 F8
South Martin 56 D5
South Milford 22 D6
South Mud Lake 27 F7
South Park 22 F1
South Peru 33 A9
South Prong of Stotts Creek 44 E6; 45 F7
South Raub 31 H11
South Salem 41 B11
South Twin Lake 22 A4
South Wanatah 19 F11
South Washington 56 C1
South Whitley 28 C2
SOUTHEAST 57 F11
Southeast Grove 18 G6
Southeast Manor 45 C11
Southport 43 H12; 45 B8
Southwest 21 D10
Southwood 42 F5
Spades 53 A8
Sparksville 51 H7
SPARTA 22 G2; 53 C9
Sparta 53 C9
Spartanburg 41 D11
Spear Lake 22 G2
Spearsville 45 G7
Speed 58 F6
Speedway 38 H6
Speedway Airport 38 H5
Speicherville 27 G12
Spelterville 42 D5
SPENCER 23 H11; 51 E12; 52 E1; 58 H1; 63 A12; 64 A1
Spencer 43 H12
Spencerville 23 H10
Spencerville Bridge 23 H11
SPICE VALLEY 50 H2; 57 A8
SPICELAND 40 H4
Spiceland 40 G4
Spickert Knob 58 G5
Spindler Ditch 29 C10
Spitlers Creek 24 G4
Splinter Ridge 59 G10
Splinter Ridge Fish and Wildlife Area 59 G10
Sponsler 49 E8
Sports Lake Campground (4600) 34 E3
Spout Spring 56 B6
Spraytown 51 E9
Spring Creek 28 A3, C2; 31 C11; 36 C3, C4; 38 C3; 42 C6; 50 F2
Spring Grove 41 G11
Spring Hill 42 F5
Spring Hills Lake 64 B4
Spring Lake 39 H11
Spring Mill State Park 57 A11
Spring Run 18 H5
Springboro 31 C12
Springersville 47 B9
SPRINGFIELD 19 A12; 22 B6; 29 A10; 47 F11
Springfield 19 A12; 60 D5
Springfield Fen Nature Preserve 20 B1
Springhill 46 F5
Springport 40 D5
Springtown 44 B2
Springville 20 B1; 50 F2
Spurgeon 61 B9
Spurgeons Corner 51 D8
Squaw Creek 61 D11
Squirrel Creek 27 E10
St Anthony 56 H6
St Bernice 42 A3
St Croix 63 A8
St Francis College 29 C7
St Henry 62 A4
St James 61 B9
St Joe 23 H11
ST JOHN 18 E4
St John 18 F4; 61 C10
St Johns 23 H8
ST JOSEPH 29 B9
St Joseph 58 F6; 61 D8
St Joseph Hill 58 F6
St Joseph River 20 A6; 21 A11, B8; 23 H11; 29 A10, C8
St Josephs College 25 F8
St Leon 47 H10
St Louis Crossing 45 H11
St Marks 56 H6
St Mary-of-the-Woods College 42 E4
ST MARYS 29 H11; 35 A11
St Marys 47 G8; 58 G5
St Marys College 20 A6
St Marys River 29 D8, F9, G10, H12
St Maurice 46 G5
St Meinrad 62 B6
St Meinrad School of Theology 62 B6
St Omer 46 F2
St Paul 46 F2
St Peter 47 H9
St Phillip 61 E7
St Thomas 55 C9
St Wendel 61 C7
Stacer 61 B9
STAFFORD 23 F11; 49 E7
Stafford Center 23 F12
STAMPERS CREEK 57 D11
Stampers Creek 57 D11
Stampers Creek 57 D11
Standard 48 B5
Stanfield Lake 51 F12
Stanford 50 C1
Stanley 61 B11
Star City 26 E3
Star Mill 22 A4
Starke County Airport 20 G2
Starlight 58 F5
Starve Hollow 51 H9
Starve Hollow Lake 51 H9
Starve Hollow State Recreation Area 51 H9
State Capitol 39 H8
State Fairgrounds (4610) 39 G8
State Line 20 A6
State Line City 36 B3
State Museum 39 H8
Staunton 43 E7
Stavetown 47 F9
Steam Corner 37 D7
Stearleyville 43 F9
STEELE 49 H7; 56 A1
Steele Nature Preserve 50 C5
STEEN 55 B11
Steinbarger Lake 22 E5
Stemm 50 E3
Stendal 56 H2
Stephens Creek 50 B4
Stephens Crossing 37 B7
STERLING 57 G10
Sterling Heights 44 A6
STEUBEN 23 D9; 30 H4; 36 A4
Steubenville 23 D9
Stevenson 61 E10
Stewart 30 G4
Stewartsville 60 B6
Stilesville 44 C2
Stillwater Creek 37 E8
Stillwell 20 D2
Stinesville 44 H2
Stinking Fork of Little Blue River 63 A9, B10
Stock Ditch 21 E7
Stockdale 27 F10
Stockheughter Bridge 46 G6
Stockport 34 H4
STOCKTON 49 D7
Stockton 49 A9
Stockwell 31 H12
Stokey Ridge 49 B11
Stone 41 A9
Stone Bluff 36 B6
Stone Head 51 C8
Stone Lake 22 A2
Stone Quarry Mills 40 G4
Stones Crossing 45 D8
STONEY CREEK 41 B7
Stoney Creek 41 C7
Stoney Creek Golf Course 39 D10
Stonington 57 A11
STONY CREEK 39 D11; 40 D6
Stony Creek 22 D2
Stony Creek 22 D1; 28 C3; 39 D10, D11
Stony Lonesome 51 B9
Stony Run 18 G6
Storks Ferry 55 B12
Story 51 C7
Story Lake 23 E8
Stotts Creek 44 E6
Stout Creek 50 A3
Stout Ditch 26 E1
Stoutsburg 25 B8
Stoutsburg Savanna Nature Preserve 25 B8
Stowers Ditch 38 A5
Straley Hill 43 H12
Strangers Brook 43 B8
Straughn 40 H6
Strawtown 39 C10
Stringtown 38 C4; 61 D9
Stroh 23 C7
Strole Ditch 24 G5
Stucker Ditch 58 A5
Stucker Fork of Stucker Ditch 59 B7
Studebaker National Museum 20 B6
Stump Ditch 32 G5
Stumpke Corner 53 B8
SUGAR CREEK 37 B12; 38 A6, B1; 39 H10; 42 E3; 45 A10, D10
Sugar Creek 45 C11
Sugar Creek 28 D3; 30 B4, B5; 31 E12; 32 E1, E2; 33 D10; 36 G5, G6; 37 C11, E9, E10, F8; 38 A6, B4, C1, C2; 39 F12, G12; 40 D3, F1, F2; 45 A11, C10, F10, G9; 48 B4; 52 B4; 55 F12; 56 C4, D4; 57 A11; 62 A3
Sugar Creek Campground (4620) 38 C3
Sugar Grove 64 C5
Sugar Grove Winery 44 C5
Sugar Mill Creek 37 F7
Sugar Mill Lake 37 D8
SUGAR RIDGE 43 G8
Sugar Ridge Fish and Wildlife Area 55 F12; 56 G1, H1; 62 A1
Sugar Ridge Golf Club 53 B12
Suicide Cave 58 B2
Sullivan 48 C5
Sullivan County Airport 48 C4
Sulphur 63 A10
Sulphur Creek 48 B6; 50 G1
Sulphur Fork Creek 63 C7
Sulphur Spring 57 A7; 64 A2
Sulphur Springs 40 E4; 63 A10
Sulphur Springs 49 H12; 58 D2
Sultan's Run Golf Course 56 F5
Suman 19 D10
Sumava Resorts 24 B4
Summers Campground (4630) 30 F6
Summit 19 B12; 23 E9; 49 D7
Summit Chapel 27 A8
Summit Grove 42 A5
Summit Lake 40 D6
Summit Lake State Park 40 D6
Summitville 34 G2
Sundown Manor 44 C5
Sunman 53 A8
Sunny Slopes 50 C3
Sunnybrook Acres 29 B9
Sunnymeadow 29 C8
Sunnymede 27 H11
Sunnymede Woods 29 D9
Sunrise Beach 22 F1
Sunrise Golf Course 59 A11
Sunset Hill 43 E12
Sunset Village 59 E9
Sunshine Gardens 45 B7
Surprise 51 E9
Surrey 25 E7
Survant 56 G2
Sutton Ridge 53 B10
Swalls 42 E6
Swamp Creek 32 H6
Swamp Rose Nature Preserve 20 D6
SWAN 22 H6
Swan 23 H7
Swan Pond Ditch 55 C9, D8
Swanington 30 C6
Swank Creek 27 D12
Swanville 59 B9
Swartz Ditch 23 F9
Swayzee 33 E12
Swede Lake 19 C12
Sweetser 33 D12
Sweetwater Lake 45 H8
Swingle Ditch 26 F1
Switz City 49 D9
Sycamore 33 E10
Sycamore Corner 30 G4
Sycamore Creek 23 G7; 44 D4
Sycamore Golf Course 28 E1
Sylvan Lake 22 E5
Sylvan Manor 19 E8
Sylvania 36 F6
Symonds Creek 41 F7
Symons Creek 40 G6; 41 H7
Syndicate 42 C5
Syracuse 21 F12
Syracuse Lake 22 F1
Syria 57 C11

T

T C Steele State Historic Site 50 C5
Tab 30 F4
Tabertown 42 E6
Taggart 51 A8
Talbot 30 E4
Tall Oaks Lake 47 H8
Tall Sycamore Campground (4640) 32 A6
Talma 27 B8
Tamarack Bog 22 B6
Tamarack Bog Nature Preserve 22 B6
Tamarack Lake 22 D6; 23 A8
Tameka Woods Golf Course 45 F7
Tampico 51 H10
Tangier 36 F6
Tanner 49 D12
Tanners Creek 53 C11
Tapps Ridge 53 H9
Tarkeo Corner 52 A4
Tarry Park 50 H3
Taswell 57 G9
TAYLOR 33 F9; 43 F12; 49 F11; 64 D4
Taylor 31 G10
Taylor Corner 23 E10; 37 D9
Taylor Creek 33 D11
Taylor Ditch 20 A4
Taylor Hill 43 H12; 51 B9
Taylor Ridge 49 E11; 51 C7
Taylor University 34 E4
Taylorsville 45 H10
Taylorville 42 E4
Tea Creek 52 G1
Tecumseh 31 F11; 42 D4
Teegarden 20 E5
Tefft 25 B10
Tell City 62 F6
Temple 57 G11
Templeton 31 E7
Templeton Creek 47 D10
Tennyson 62 C2
Terhune 38 B6
Terrace Bay 32 A1
Terre Haute 42 E5
Terre Haute KOA (4650) 42 F6
Terre Vin Winery 42 F5
Terry 63 C8
Tetersburg 33 H8
Texas 53 D11
Thales 56 E6
Thayer 24 B5
Theis Creek 63 D7
Theis Ridge 63 D7
Thomas 56 C1
Thomas Family Winery 59 A11
Thomas J Miller Lake 59 B7
Thomaston 19 G12
Thompson Ditch 25 C12; 26 C1
Thompson Lake 42 F5
Thompson Mound 60 D3
Thompson Slough 51 C11
THORNCREEK 28 A3
Thornhope 26 F3
Thorntown 38 C2
Thorpe Creek 39 E11
Thorpe Ford Bridge 42 C6
Three Lakes Trail 44 H4
Threemile Creek 35 C9
Thumma Ditch 22 G6
Thunderbird Pond 48 A4
Thurman 29 C9
Tiernan Ditch 29 B9
Tige Creek 63 A8
Tighe 42 C3
Tilden 38 H4
Tillery Hill 57 F8
Tilley Ditch 48 H5
Tillman 29 D11
Timbercrest 28 D6
Timberhurst 23 D7
Time Corners 29 D7
Timmons Ditch 26 G1
Tiosa 27 B7
TIPPECANOE 21 G12; 22 H1; 26 C3; 27 A8; 31 D11; 32 C1
Tippecanoe 27 A8
Tippecanoe Battlefield National Historic Landmark 31 E11
Tippecanoe Country Club 25 H12
Tippecanoe Lake 21 G12
Tippecanoe River 21 H12; 25 G12; 26 B3, C5, E2, G1; 27 A9, A11, C7; 31 A12, D12; 32 C1
Tippecanoe River Nature Preserve 26 C3
Tippecanoe River State Park 26 C2
Tipsaw Lake 63 C8
TIPTON 33 B7
Tipton 33 H9
Titus 63 D12
TOBIN 63 F8
Tobinsport 63 G8
Tocsin 29 G8
Todd Ditch 33 G12
Toledo 28 H5
Toliver Hollow 57 C9
Toll Gate Heights 35 A8
Toney Ditch 32 B6
Topeka 22 D3
Toto 26 A1
Tough Creek 45 H12
Town Creek 59 B8
Town of Pines 19 B10
Townley 29 D11
Tracy 20 E1
Traders Point 38 F6
Trafalgar 45 F8
Trail Creek 19 A11
Tratebas Mill 19 D9
Travis Ditch 20 E1
Travis Hill 45 D7
Travisville 35 B7
Treaty 33 A12
Tree Spring 36 C4
Tremont 19 B9; 38 H6
Trenton 35 F7
Trevlac 50 A5
Tri Lakes 28 A4
Tri-County Fish and Wildlife Area 22 G1
Tri-County Golf Club 40 D4
Tri-State University 23 C9
Tri-State–Steuben County Airport 23 C8
Trier Ditch 29 D8
Trimble Creek 27 A10, C11
Trimer 32 A4
Trimmer Hill 42 G6
Trinity 35 D11
Trinity Springs 56 A6
Trotter Crossing 57 E11
TROY 23 E11; 36 B5; 63 E7
Troy 62 E6
Troy Cedar Lake 28 A3
Tucker Lake 57 E9
Tulip 49 C11
Tully Ditch 24 A6
Tunker 28 D3
Tunnel Falls 59 A10
Tunnelton 50 H5
TURKEY CREEK 21 G12; 22 G1
Turkey Creek 23 D7
Turkey Creek 18 E4, E6; 21 E11, F11, F12; 23 C7; 33 G10, H8
Turkey Creek Meadows 18 E5
Turkey Fork of Little Blue River 63 A11, B11
Turkey Hill 45 E7; 55 G12
Turkey Ridge Trail 63 B12
Turkey Run 37 B7
Turkey Run State Park 37 F7, G7
Turkey Track 44 G4
TURMAN 48 C3
Turman Creek 42 H5; 48 A5, B4, C2
Turner 43 E8
Turpin Hill 61 B12
Turtle Creek 48 C3
Turtle Creek Reservoir 48 D3
Twelve Mile 27 G7
Twelve Mile Creek 27 H7
Twelve Points 42 E5
Twin Beach 43 D7
Twin Bridges 55 D8
Twin Bridges Golf Club 44 A3
Twin Creek 57 A12
Twin Hills 35 E8
Twin Lake 48 E6
Twin Lakes 20 H5; 22 A4
Twin Lakes 20 A5
Twin Mills Resort (4660) 22 A4
Twin Swamps Nature Preserve 60 H4
Twomile Ditch 35 E7
Tyler Ditch 25 A7
Tyner 20 F5
Tyner Crossing 47 B7

U

Ulen 38 D4
Underwood 58 C6
Underwood Hollow 57 E10
UNION 19 E7; 20 E1, E6; 21 D7, E10; 23 G9; 25 D7, H12; 26 A5, D4, H1; 27 F8; 28 C5, G5, G6; 29 F11; 30 B6; 31 A12, G10; 32 A1, G3; 33 F11; 34 G5; 37 C11, H9; 38 D6, G3; 40 C2; 41 D8; 43 A9; 45 E7; 46 B5, C1; 47 D11; 53 E10; 55 H8; 57 H9; 58 E6; 61 A9, G8; 63 A9, C9
Union 45 H9; 51 A9; 55 E10
Union Center 20 E2
Union City 41 A12
Union Mills 19 E12
Union Tar Spring 63 A9
Uniondale 29 G7
Unionport 41 C8
Uniontown 51 G12; 63 A8
Unionville 50 A5
Universal 42 C4
University Heights 45 A8
University of Evansville 61 E9
University of Indianapolis 45 A8
University of Notre Dame 21 B7
University of Southern Indiana 61 E7
Upland 34 E4
Upper Basin 23 A9
Upper Fish Lake 20 D3
Upper Indian Creek 53 H9
Upper Long Lake 22 G4
Upper River Deshee 55 C11
Upper Sulphur Creek 57 D9
Upper Sunset Park 31 A12
Upton 60 E4
Urbana 27 F12
Urmeyville 45 D10
Utah 53 D11
UTICA 59 G7
Utica 59 G8

V

Valeene 57 F11
Valentine 22 C5
Valle Vista Country Club 45 C8
Valley Brook 27 H11
Valley City 64 C1
Valley Mills 44 B6
Valley View Golf Course 40 D3
Vallonia 51 G8
Valparaiso 19 E9
Valparaiso University 19 E9
VAN BUREN 21 G11; 22 A2; 26 E3; 34 C3, G2; 36 B6; 43 D8; 45 B12; 49 H10; 50 C2; 51 C8; 56 A4
Van Buren 34 C3
Van Buren Park 50 C3
Van Nuys 40 E5

continue on next page

🌲 State Lands

NAME, LOCATION	PAGE & GRID	ACREAGE
Bass Lake State Beach, Bass Lake	26 A3	21
Brown County State Park, Nashville	51 B7	15,696
Chain O'Lakes State Park, Burr Oak	22 G5	2,678
Charlestown State Park, Charlestown	59 F8	2,300
Clark State Forest, Henryville	58 D6	23,979
Clifty Falls State Park, Madison	59 A10	1,361
Deam Lake State Recreation Area, Carwood	58 E5	1,300
Falls of the Ohio State Park, Jeffersonville	58 H6	68
Ferdinand State Forest, Ferdinand	63 A7	7,657
Ft Harrison State Park, Indianapolis	39 G9	1,700
Greene–Sullivan State Forest, Dugger	48 D6	7,964
Hardy Lake State Recreation Area, New Frankfort	52 H1	1,321
Harmonie State Park, New Harmony	60 C4	3,465
Harrison–Crawford/Wyandotte Complex, Leavenworth	63 B12	23,644
Indiana Dunes State Park, Dune Acres	19 B9	2,182
Jackson–Washington State Forest, Brownstown	51 G9	15,721
Lincoln State Park, Lincoln City	62 C4	1,747
Martin State Forest, Willow Valley	57 B7	7,023
McCormicks Creek State Park, Spencer	44 H1	1,833
Morgan–Monroe State Forest, Hindustan	44 H4	23,680
Ouabache State Park, Bluffton	35 A8	1,104
Owen–Putnam State Forest, Vandalia	43 H11	6,245
Pokagon State Park, Lake James	23 A9	1,203
Potato Creek State Park, North Liberty	20 D5	3,840
Selmier State Forest, North Vernon	52 D2	355
Shades State Park, Alamo	37 F9	3,082
Shakamak State Park, Jasonville	49 B7	1,766
Starve Hollow State Recreation Area, Vallonia	51 H9	500
Summit Lake State Park, Rogersville	40 D6	2,680
Tippecanoe River State Park, Beardstown	26 C2	2,761
Turkey Run State Park, Marshall	37 G7	2,382
Versailles State Park, Versailles	53 D7	5,905
White River State Park, Indianapolis	45 A7	250
Whitewater Memorial State Park, Liberty	47 C10	1,710
Yellowwood State Forest, Belmont	50 B5	23,326

Facility/Recreation columns (FACILITIES: Bathhouse, Cabins/Cottages, Dumping Station, Road Stand, Group Facilities, Nature Center, Swimming Area, Tennis Courts, Visitor Center; RECREATION: Boating, Camping, Fishing, Hiking, Horseback Riding, Cross-Country Skiing, Swimming) are indicated by bullet marks in the source table.

NAME, LOCATION	PAGE & GRID	ACREAGE	ADMINISTRATION	FACILITIES — DUMPING STATION	MARINA	RECREATION — PICNIC AREA	VISITOR CENTER	BOATING	CAMPING	FISHING	HIKING	SWIMMING
Brookville Lake Project, Brookville	47 F10	16,445	USACE	●	●	●	●	●	●	●	●	●
Cagles Mill Lake Project, Poland	43 E11	8,075	USACE	●	●	●		●	●	●	●	●
Cannelton Locks and Dam Project, Cannelton	63 F7	8,339	USACE			●		●		●		
Cecil M Harden Lake Project, Ferndale	43 A9	4,065	USACE	●	●	●	●	●	●	●	●	●
Falls of the Ohio National Wildlife Conservation Area, Jeffersonville	58 H6	1,404	USACE			●	●			●	●	
Hoosier National Forest, Huron	63 F8	193,000	USFS	●	●	●	●	●	●	●	●	●
Indiana Dunes National Lakeshore, Porter	19 C8	12,818	NPS			●	●	●	●	●	●	●
J Edward Roush Lake Project, Huntington	28 G4	8,217	USACE			●		●	●	●	●	
John T Myers Locks and Dam Project, Hovey	60 H4	7,900	USACE			●		●		●		
Mississinewa Lake Project, Peoria	33 A10	14,386	USACE	●	●	●		●	●	●	●	●
Monroe Lake Project, Guthrie	50 E3	23,952	USACE	●	●	●	●	●	●	●	●	●
Muscatatuck National Wildlife Refuge, Seymour	51 E12	7,802	USFWS			●	●			●	●	
Newburgh Locks and Dam Project, Newburgh	61 F11	354	USACE			●		●		●		
Patoka Lake Project, Cuzco	57 F7	25,583	USACE	●	●	●	●	●	●	●	●	●
Patoka River National Wildlife Refuge and Management Area, Oakland City	55 G12	2,100	USFWS							●		
Salamonie Lake Project, Largo	28 H1	12,300	USACE	●	●	●	●	●	●	●	●	●

Covered Bridges

NAME, LOCATION	PAGE & GRID	SPANS	STRUCTURE	LENGTH (feet)	YEAR CONSTRUCTED
Adams Mill Bridge, Cutler	32 E3	Wildcat Creek	HT	138	1872
Bakers Camp Bridge, Bainbridge	43 A12	Big Walnut Creek	BA	128	1901
Bean Blossom Bridge, Bean Blossom	50 A6	Bean Blossom Creek	HT	60	1880
Beeson Bridge, Rockville	43 A7	—	BA	55	1906
Bells Ford Bridge, Seymour	51 E10	East Fork of White River	PT	330	1869
Big Rocky Fork Bridge, Mansfield	43 B9	Big Rocky Fork Creek	BA	72	1900
Billie Creek Bridge, Rockville	43 A7	Williams Creek	BA	62	1895
Bowsher Ford Bridge, Howard	36 F5	Mill Creek	BA	72	1915
Bridgeton Bridge, Bridgeton	43 B7	Big Raccoon Creek	BA	245	1868
Busching Bridge, Versailles	53 D7	Laughery Creek	HT	176	1885
Cades Mill Bridge, Steam Corner	36 D6	Coal Creek	HT	150	1854
Cataract Falls Bridge, Cataract	43 F12	Mill Creek	ST	140	1876
Catlin Bridge, Rockville	37 H7	Bill Diddle Creek	BA	54	1907
Cedar Chapel Bridge, Fishers	39 E9	—	HT	112	1884
Ceylon Bridge, Ceylon	35 C10	Wabash River	HT	126	1862
Conleys Ford Bridge, Walton	43 B8	Big Raccoon Creek	BA	192	1907
Cornstalk Bridge, Raccoon	37 G11	Cornstalk Creek	BA	82	1917
Cox Ford Bridge, Annapolis	37 G7	Sugar Creek	BA	176	1913
Crooks Bridge, Rockville	43 A7	Little Raccoon Creek	BA	132	1856
Crown Point Bridge, Crown Point	18 F5	—	BA	85	1878
Cumberland Bridge, Matthews	34 G4	Mississinewa River	HT	175	1877
Darlington Bridge, Darlington	37 C12	Sugar Creek	HT	140	1868
Deers Mill Bridge, Deer Mill	37 F9	Sugar Creek	BA	275	1878
Dick Huffman Bridge, Reelsville	43 E10	Big Walnut Creek	HT	265	1880
Dunbar Bridge, Greencastle	43 B11	Big Walnut Creek	BA	174	1880
Edna Collins Bridge, Clinton Falls	43 A10	Little Walnut Creek	BA	80	1922
Eugene Bridge, Eugene	36 E4	Vermillion River	BA	192	1885
Forsythe Mill Bridge, Gowdy	46 D3	Big Flat Rock River	BA	196	1888
Guilford Bridge, Guilford	53 B11	—	BA	104	1879
Harry Evans Bridge, Coxville	42 B6	Rock Run Creek	BA	65	1908
Hillsdale Bridge, Dana	36 H4	—	BA	104	1876
Holton Bridge, Holton	52 C5	Otter Creek	HT	112	1884
Houck Bridge, Manhattan	43 C10	Big Walnut Creek	HT	210	1880
Huffman Mill Bridge, Huffman	62 C6	Anderson River	BA	140	1884
Irishman Bridge, Youngstown	42 G5	Fowler Lake	QP	75	circa 1847
Jackson Bridge, Rockport	36 G6	Sugar Creek	BA	207	1861
James Bridge, Lovett	52 F2	Big Graham Creek	HT	124	1887
Lancaster Bridge, Owasco	32 E2	Wildcat Creek	HT	133	1872
Leatherwood Station Bridge, Rockville	43 A7	—	BA	72	1899
Longwood Bridge, Connersville	47 B8	—	BA	92	1884
Mansfield Bridge, Mansfield	43 B8	Big Raccoon Creek	BA	247	1867
Marshall Bridge, Rockport	36 G6	Rush Creek	BA	56	1917
McAllister Bridge, Catlin	43 A7	Little Raccoon Creek	BA	126	1914
Mecca Bridge, Mecca	42 A6	Big Raccoon Creek	BA	150	1873
Medora Bridge, Medora	51 H8	East Fork of White River	BA	434	1875
Melcher Bridge, Melcher	36 H5	Leatherwood Creek	BA	83	1896
Mill Creek–Tow Path Bridge, Howard	36 F5	Mill Creek	BA	92	1907
Moscow Bridge, Moscow	46 E3	Big Flat Rock River	BA	334	1886
Narrows Bridge, Marshall	37 G7	Sugar Creek	BA	121	1882
Neet Bridge, Catlin	43 B7	Little Raccoon Creek	BA	126	1904
Nevins Bridge, Minshall	43 B7	Little Raccoon Creek	BA	155	1920
New Brownsville Bridge, Columbus	51 A10	Mill Run Creek	LT	93	1840
Newport Bridge, Newport	36 G4	Little Vermillion River	BA	180	1885
Norris Ford Bridge, Rushville	46 B5	Big Flat Rock River	BA	169	1916
North Manchester Bridge, North Manchester	27 E12	Eel River	ST	150	1872
Oakalla Bridge, Greencastle	43 C10	Big Walnut Creek	BA	152	1898
Offutt Ford Bridge, Henderson	46 B3	Little Blue River	BA	98	1884
Old Red Bridge, Jimtown	60 A5	Big Bayou Creek	ST	170	1875
Phillips Bridge, Arabia	36 H6	Big Pond Creek	KP	43	1909
Pine Bluff Bridge, Carpentersville	37 H12	Big Walnut Creek	HT	211	unknown
Portland Mills Bridge, Guion	37 G8	Little Raccoon Creek	BA	130	1856
Potters Bridge, Noblesville	39 D9	West Fork of White River	HT	259	1871
Ramp Creek Bridge, Nashville	51 B7	Salt Creek	BA	96	1838
Richland Creek Bridge, Bloomfield	49 E10	Richland Creek	BA	100	1883
Roann Bridge, Roann	27 F10	Eel River	HT	288	1872
Rob Roy Bridge, Rob Roy	37 A7	Big Shawnee Creek	HT	120	1860
Rollingstone Bridge, Bainbridge	37 H12	Big Walnut Creek	BA	103	1915
Roseville Bridge, Coxville	42 B6	Big Raccoon Creek	BA	263	1910
Rush Creek Bridge, Tangier	36 F6	Rush Creek	BA	77	1904
Scipio Bridge, Scipio	52 C1	Sand Creek	HT	146	1886
Shieldstown Bridge, Shields	51 F9	East Fork of White River	BA	331	1876
Sim Smith Bridge, Arabia	36 H6	Leatherwood Creek	BA	84	1883
Smith Bridge, Rushville	46 C5	Big Flat Rock River	BA	138	1877
Snow Hill Bridge, Rockdale	47 H11	Johnson Fork of Whitewater Creek	HT	75	1894
Spencerville Bridge, Spencerville	23 H11	St Joseph River	HT	160	1873
Stockheughter Bridge, Enochsburg	46 G6	Salt Creek	HT	92	1887
Thorpe Ford Bridge, Rosedale	42 C6	Big Raccoon Creek	BA	163	1912
Vermont Bridge, Kokomo	33 E8	Kokomo Creek	ST	98	1875
Wallace Bridge, Wallace	37 E8	Sugar Mill Creek	HT	81	1871
West Union Bridge, West Union	36 G5	Sugar Creek	BA	315	1876
Westport Bridge, Westport	52 B3	Sand Creek	BA	115	1880
Wheeling Bridge, Oatsville	55 F10	Patoka River	ST	164	1877
Whitewater Canal Aqueduct Bridge, Metamora	47 F8	Duck Creek	BA	81	1846
Wilkens Mill Bridge, Annapolis	37 F7	Sugar Mill Creek	BA	102	1906
Williams Bridge, Williams	50 H2	East Fork of White River	HT	376	1884
Zacke Cox Bridge, Mecca	42 B6	Rock Run	BA	54	1908

Nature Preserves

Since 1969, over 20,000 acres of state-owned land in Indiana have been designated as protected nature preserves, representing the most widely distributed system of protected lands in the state. Due to prohibited or restricted public access, some nature preserves are not included in this chart.

NAME, LOCATION	PAGE & GRID	ACREAGE	COMMENTS
Baltzell–Lenhart Woods Nature Preserve, Decatur	29 H10	37	Mesic and wet–mesic flatwoods; old-growth stand. Mainly oaks and hickories with swamp white oaks, red maples, sycamores and cottonwoods.
Berns–Meyer Nature Preserve, Pulaski	26 E2	20	Mixed mesophytic woodland with red oak, white oak, tulip and shagbark hickory trees. Spring wildflowers such as marsh marigold and green dragon. Trails.
Big Chapman Lake Nature Preserve, Warsaw	21 H12	147	Cattail marsh, bog and marl-beach prairie. Marsh is feeding and nesting area for water birds such as bitterns, herons and rails.
Big Spring Nature Preserve, Palmyra	58 E2	10	Alluviated cave spring. Water supply originates from sinkhole plain to northeast of site; minimum flow reported at 650,000 gallons per day. Trail.
Bloomfield Barrens Nature Preserve, Bloomfield	62 D2	466	Flats with sparse tree cover, dominated by rushes, grasses, lichens and mosses. Post oak tree population.
Brock–Sampson Nature Preserve, Bridgeport	64 A5	453	Example of terrain known as knobs: high ridge tops and deep ravines. Dry habitat with bedrock outcrops. Little bluestem, poverty grass. Views of Ohio River valley.
Bryan Nature Preserve, Hamilton	32 G2	29	Patch of old-growth woods stands out amidst farmland. Tall, dense forest canopy includes great white oaks 4 feet in diameter. Trail.
Clifty Canyon Nature Preserve, Clifty Falls State Park	59 A10	179	Streams cut deep gorges into ancient Ordovician rock beds (exposing fossils) and tumble over spectacular waterfalls. Trails.
Conrad Savanna Nature Preserve, Lake Village	24 C4	313	Open savanna of broad flats and rolling hills; soil of fine quartz sand. Black and white oak trees common. Plants include goat's rue, milkweed and leadplant.
Crooked Lake Nature Preserve, Merriam	28 A4	100	Undeveloped shoreline on one of state's deepest lakes. Forested slopes; wetland habitats; island in lake. Trails.
Dogwood Nature Preserve, Versailles State Park	53 D7	20	Small, undisturbed old-growth stand of hardwoods grows on cool, north-facing slope. Named for prominent flowering dogwood. Naturalist on site in summer.
Donaldson Cave/Donaldsons Woods Nature Preserve, Spring Mill State Park	57 A11	73	Picturesque area features stream flowing from cave mouth to gorge bottom. Nearby is one of last remaining stands of state's original forest. Trails.
Dunes Nature Preserve, Indiana Dunes State Park	19 B9	1,530	Strong winds from north and west sculpted famous dunescape along Lake Michigan shore. South of dunes is wetland area, drained by Dunes Creek. Trails.
Falling Timber Nature Preserve, Versailles State Park	53 C7	202	Mesic and dry–mesic upland forest, riparian forest and limestone glades. Rare wavy-leaf aster and threatened white gentian occur here. Trail.
Hall Woods Nature Preserve, Bainbridge	43 A12	385	Mesic upland forest with floodplain forest. Many ravines. Silver maple, buckeye and tulip trees. Abundance of large white oak. Trail.
Hemlock Bluff Nature Preserve, Leesville	50 G6	44	Located on steep slope along Guthrie Creek. Mixed stands of hemlock and hardwood trees. Features largest hemlock in state at 33 inches in diameter. Trail.
Hemmer Woods Nature Preserve, Buckskin	61 A11	73	Old-growth oak–hickory forest exemplifies original southwestern Indiana woodlands. One of state's best examples of forest with southern affinities. Trail.
Hoosier Prairie Nature Preserve, Indiana Dunes National Lakeshore	18 D4	430	Exceptionally diverse remnant prairie made up of sand plains, sedge meadows and marshes. Attracts rare animal species whose native habitats have disappeared. Trail.
Hornbeam Nature Preserve, Whitewater Memorial State Park	47 C10	83	Mesophytic hardwood forest contains unusually high number of hornbeams (blue beeches) and hop hornbeams (ironwoods). Spring wildflowers carpet forest floor. Trails.
Jug Rock Nature Preserve, Shoals	56 B6	34	Jug-shaped sandstone column stands 50 feet high. Sandstone cliff extends 160 feet above White River floodplain, affording dramatic view of valley.
Koontz Lake Nature Preserve, Koontz Lake	20 F4	148	Upland areas and savanna feature black oak trees and blueberries. Lowland communities of marsh and shrub bogs; remnant stands of tamarack.
Laketon Bog Nature Preserve, Laketon	27 E12	32	Peat-filled bog supplied by seepage from base of bluff near Eel River. Remnant stands of tamarack. Also shrub swamp, marsh and floodplain forest. Boardwalk.
Laughery Bluff Nature Preserve, Versailles State Park	53 D7	81	Preserve includes bluff-top forest, steep slopes and Laughery Creek floodplain. Exposed Silurian-age fossils reveal animals that lived in prehistoric inland sea.
Lincolns Woods Nature Preserve, Lincoln State Park	62 C4	110	Three different community types include dry, mesic and dry–mesic upland forests. Post, blackjack and black oaks dominate presettlement-condition dry portion. Trail.
Little Chapman Lake Nature Preserve, Warsaw	21 H12	82	Northern half is primarily cattail marsh. Southern half features bog with unusual species such as pitcher plant and cranberries.
Liverpool Nature Preserve, Lake Station	18 D6	20	Western half is sand savanna that grades into prairie to east. Acidic sand exposed by past sand mining operations. Revegetated with various rare plants.
Loon Lake Nature Preserve, Angola	23 B9	99	Several wetland communities home to many rare, threatened or endangered plant species. These include bladderwort, cuckoo flower and pitcher plant. Trail.
Lubbe Nature Preserve, Farmers Retreat	53 E8	34	One of Dearborn County's highest elevations is dominated by beech, maple, ash, oak and hickory forest. Understory species include devil's club and leatherwood.
Manitou Islands Wetland Conservation Area and Nature Preserve, Rochester	27 D7	298	Marsh wrens, rails, ducks, herons, red-winged blackbirds and swamp sparrows flock to wetland communities of cattails, lily pads and bulrushes. Forested islands.
Moraine Nature Preserve, Valparaiso	19 D9	474	Topography exemplifies Valparaiso Moraine—formed by southern edge of Lake Michigan lobe of Wisconsin glaciation. Ridges, potholes and grassy fields. Trails.
Nine Penny Branch Nature Preserve, Charlestown	59 E8	121	Old-growth mesic upland forest bisected by Nine Penny Branch of Fourteenmile Creek. Ravine carved into limestone bedrock. Waterfalls and pools. Early stagecoach route followed stream.
Ogle Hollow Nature Preserve, Brown County State Park	51 B7	41	One of few places in state where rare yellowwood tree found. Cool, moist slope also supports dogwood, red bud variety of ferns. Naturalist on site year-round. Trail.
Olin Lake Nature Preserve, Wolcottville	22 D5	269	At over 100 acres, Olin Lake is largest lake in Indiana with undeveloped shoreline. Swamp forest and skunk cabbage along marshy shore. Trail.
Orangeville Rise of Lost River Nature Preserve, Orangeville	57 C9	3	Artesian spring is actually emergence of major underground tributary to Lost River. Water rises into 220-foot-wide rock-walled pit.
Pine Hills Nature Preserve, Shades State Park	37 F9	480	Rugged hills and deep gorges formed by receding glaciers. Forested areas cleared for timber during 19th century allowed to return to original state. Trails.
Pipewort Pond Nature Preserve, Bristol	21 A12	135	Shallow pond with seasonal water fluctuations attracts herons, ducks and shorebirds. Disjunct Atlantic Coastal Plain plants include umbrella sage and pipewort.
Portland Arch Nature Preserve, Fountain	36 A5	293	Bear Creek tributary carved opening through massive sandstone, creating natural bridge. Vertical cliff faces support variety of ferns. Trail.
Potawatomi Nature Preserve, Pokagon State Park	23 A9	256	Natural lake, cattail marshes, sedge meadows, and tamarack and yellow birch swamps exemplify original northeastern morainal topography. Trails.
Rocky Hollow–Falls Canyon Nature Preserve, Turkey Run State Park	37 F7	1,609	Sandstone walls, covered with ferns and hydrangeas, flank narrow canyons. Terraces along Sugar Creek covered with old-growth forest. Waterfalls. Trails.
Round Lake Wetland Conservation Area and Nature Preserve, Bass Lake	26 A2	140	Round Lake shoreline and surrounding wetlands nurture cattails and floating sedge marsh. Uplands on southwestern portion of reserve once farmed.
Sandhill Nature Preserve, Tippecanoe River State Park	26 B2	120	Sand hills were created by glacial outwash stream deposits. Winds reworked sand into rolling dunes and flat plains. Prairie vegetation. Trail.
Shrader–Weaver Nature Preserve, Bentonville	47 A7	96	Site contains pioneer homestead, fields and 28 acres of beech–maple old-growth forest. Large specimens of tulip, wild black cherry and black walnut trees. Trails.
Springfield Fen Nature Preserve, Springville	20 B1	45	Prairie fen contains rare prairie grasses and herbs. Ridge overlooks fen. Year-round springs flow at base of ridge.
Steele Nature Preserve, T C Steele State Historic Site	50 C5	92	Mesic and dry-mesic upland forest and two deep ravines contain intermittent streams. Wildflowers include orchid and whorled pogonia. Trails.
Stoutsburg Savanna Nature Preserve, Wheatfield	25 B8	236	Rolling sand ridges deposited by glacial meltwaters typify Kankakee River valley. Rare plant species include silky aster, cream wild indigo and sweet fern.
Swamp Rose Nature Preserve, Potato Creek State Park	20 D6	100	Round hills and low outwashes formed by receding glaciers. Once-pastured lowland now reverting to shrub swamp. Swamp rose. Year-round naturalist on site.
Tamarack Bog Nature Preserve, Pigeon River Fish and Wildlife Area	22 B6	170	Largest remaining tamarack tree swamp (more typical of northern states and Canada) in state. Cool microclimate supports rare and endangered plants and animals.
Tippecanoe River Nature Preserve, Tippecanoe River State Park	26 C3	180	Floodplain and bottomland areas adjacent to river contain several oxbow sloughs. Habitats support great blue herons, prothonotary warblers, beaver and mink. Trails.
Twin Swamps Nature Preserve, Hovey	60 H4	598	Rare remnant of swamp cottonwood–bald cypress and overcup oak swamps separated by southern flatwoods, which once covered Ohio and Wabash river valleys. Trail.
Versailles Flatwoods Nature Preserve, Versailles SP	53 D7	45	Significant example of mesic flatwoods typical of southeastern Indiana. Vernal pools contain species typical of floodplains.
Wawasee Wetlands Nature Preserve, Wawasee	22 F1	17	Preserve contains cattail marsh, sedge meadow and small island. Marsh biodiversity helps protect water quality of adjacent Lake Wawasee. Access via Johnson Bay only.
Wells Woods Nature Preserve, Commiskey	52 G2	20	Old-growth forest situated on what locals call "white clay flats" (Cobbsfork silt loam soil). Spring ponds dry to point of cracking in summer.
Wesselman Woods Nature Preserve, Evansville	61 E9	197	Wide diversity of trees, shrubs and wildflowers within old-growth forest. Unique for southern influences (sugarberry and cherrybark oak). Trails.
Wolf Cave Nature Preserve, McCormicks Creek State Park	44 H1	214	Small underground water passage for wet-weather stream. Natural bridge located where water emerges. Diverse forest habitat. Trail.
Yellow Birch Ravine Nature Preserve, Taswell	57 H9	441	System of ravines viewed from uplands or cliff-lined ravine bottoms. Only place in southern Indiana where yellow birch, hemlock and mountain laurel found together.

Wineries

NAME, LOCATION	PAGE & GRID	COMMENTS
Anderson's Orchard & Winery, Valparaiso	19 D10	Fruit winery and family-owned farm offers homemade goods in addition to orchard and winery tours. Wine tasting.
Borns Winery, Madison	59 A11	Owned by descendant of German winemaking family. Wines from fruit and French hybrid and native American grapes. Wine tasting.
Brown County Winery, Nashville	51 A7	Family-owned winery specializes in fruit wines. Also offers five grape varieties. Wine tasting.
Butler Winery, Bloomington	50 B3	Dinner wines made from Indiana-grown grapes. Specialty foods in outdoor garden. Cellar tours. Wine tasting.
Chateau Pomije, New Alsace	53 A10	Scenic 50-acre vineyard among rolling hills. Winery in renovated 1891 barn. Wine tasting.
Chateau Thomas Winery, Plainfield	44 B5	Offers twelve premium vinifera wines. Specialty foods. Wine tasting.
Easley Winery, Indianapolis	39 H8	Family-run winery has produced wine from French hybrid and native American grapes for 20 years. Grapes grown in vineyard along Ohio River. Wine tasting.
French Lick Winery & Coffee Company, French Lick	57 D8	Eighteen grape and fruit wines. Housed in Beechwood Mansion. Specialty foods. Cellar tours. Wine tasting.
Gaia Wines, Indianapolis	39 H8	Winery features 10 wines, Indiana winemaking history and monthly events. Specialty foods. Tours. Wine tasting.
Huber Orchard and Winery, Starlight	58 F4	Family-owned farm offers 18 styles of grape and fruit wine as well as bakery, cheese factory and petting zoo. Vineyard and winery tours. Wine tasting.
Kauffman Winery, Mt Vernon	61 F7	Only vineyard and winery in southwestern part of state produces nine estate-bottled wines. Tours by appointment.
Lake Michigan Winery, Whiting	18 B3	Produces wines from grapes grown in Ohio River valley and along Lake Michigan. Personalized labels. Specialty foods. Wine tasting.
Lanthier Winery, Madison	59 A11	Winery in 18th-century fort produces 11 fruit and grape wines and occasional specialties such as dandelion and rose petal wine. Garden. Wine tasting.
Madison Vineyards, Madison	52 H5	Five-acre vineyard grows seyval blanc and Cayuga white grapes. Vineyard and winery tours. Specialty foods. Picnic area. Wine tasting.
Oliver Winery, Bloomington	44 H3	State's largest and oldest winery produces wines from vinifera grapes. Cellar tours. Lakeside picnic area. Wine tasting.
Sugar Grove Winery, Mooresville	44 C5	Named for area's sugar maple trees, winery offers six locally made wines that range from dry to sweet. Cellar tours. Picnic area. Wine tasting.
Terre Vin Winery, Terre Haute	37 H7	Labels designed by local artists adorn bottles of four locally produced wines. Specialty foods. Wine tasting.
Thomas Family Winery, Madison	59 A11	Winery in converted 1855 stable and carriage house produces wines from grapes grown on West Coast and locally. Also fruit wines and Welsh-style hard cider. Cellar tours. Wine tasting.
Villa Milan Vineyard, Milan	53 C8	Hilltop winery in scenic Ohio River valley produces four estate-bottled wines. Wine tasting.

Attractions

BILLIE CREEK VILLAGE – Rockville – 43 A7 Re-created early 20th-century village features three covered bridges and 30 historic buildings, including restored farmhouse. Historical exhibits. Mule-drawn wagon rides. Special events.

BLUE CHIP CASINO – Michigan City – 19 A11 Casino aboard luxury ocean liner that cruises Lake Michigan. Offers over 1,200 slot machines, blackjack, craps, stud poker and roulette. Restaurants, lounge and tree-lined evening garden.

COLLEGE FOOTBALL HALL OF FAME – South Bend – 21 B7 Interactive exhibits, photographs and mementos bring to life the history and lore of college football. Galleries highlight different aspects of game. Hall of Honor. Stadium Theater. Archives and library.

EITELJORG MUSEUM – Indianapolis – 39 H7 Building considered to be work of art houses Native American and Western paintings and bronze sculptures. Works by Georgia O'Keeffe, Frederic Remington and Charles Russell. Woodcarving, basketry and pottery.

EVANSVILLE MUSEUM OF ARTS AND SCIENCE – Evansville – 61 E9 Contains works of art from 16th century to present. Planetarium, hands-on science exhibits, anthropology gallery and reproduction of 19th-century American river town. Antique steam locomotive.

FOELLINGER–FREIMANN BOTANICAL CONSERVATORY – Ft Wayne – 29 D8 Midwest's largest passive solar conservatory houses three "gardens under glass." Exotic tropical plants near cascading waterfall, Sonoran desert cacti and seasonal flower displays.

FT OUIATENON HISTORIC PARK – West Lafayette – 31 F10 Reconstructed blockhouse and trading post reflect first fortified European settlement in Indiana. Established 1717 as French military outpost and later used as trading post. Feast of Hunters' Moon event held each fall.

GRISSOM AIR MUSEUM – Bunker Hill – 33 B8 Museum presents aviation history from WWII through the Gulf War. Outdoor display includes B-17 Flying Fortress, B-58 Hustler and A-10 Warthog. Armaments, models, uniforms, engines and interactive exhibits.

INDIANA BASKETBALL HALL OF FAME – New Castle – 40 F5 Museum reflects Hoosier basketball tradition. Game films, photographs and interactive exhibits salute over 1,000 Indiana high schools and former stars such as Larry Bird, Oscar Robertson and Johnnie Wooden.

INDIANA RAILWAY MUSEUM – French Lick – 57 D8 Scenic train ride through 20 miles of Hoosier National Forest, limestone bluffs and 2,200-foot-long Burton Tunnel, one of longest railroad tunnels in state. Steam and diesel locomotives on display. Narrated tours.

INDIANA UNIVERSITY ART MUSEUM – Bloomington – 50 B3 Building designed by architect I. M. Pei houses over 30,000 works, from African masks to works by Henri Matisse, Claude Monet and Auguste Rodin. Murals by Thomas Hart Benton on display in nearby auditorium.

INDIANAPOLIS MUSEUM OF ART – Indianapolis – 39 H7 Four pavilions house permanent and changing exhibitions ranging from ancient artifacts to contemporary masterpieces. Lilly Pavilion, located in 18th-century French-style home, houses decorative arts collection. 152 landscaped acres.

JAMES DEAN GALLERY – Fairmount – 34 F2 World's largest collection of memorabilia relating to short life and career of 1950s film star, located in Dean's hometown. High school yearbooks, original movie posters and clothing from films. Guided tours. Dean's gravesite nearby.

LINCOLN MUSEUM – Ft Wayne – 29 C8 11 galleries dedicated to life and legacy of 16th US President Abraham Lincoln. Artifacts, films, historic photographs and documents signed by Lincoln. 18 interactive exhibits and four theaters.

MEDICAL HISTORY MUSEUM – Indianapolis – 39 H7 Collection of 15,000 medical and healthcare artifacts from 19th–20th century traces advent of modern, scientific medicine. Housed in 1896 Old Pathology Building. Guided tours.

MIDWEST MUSEUM OF AMERICAN ART – Elkhart – 21 B10 Divided into eight periods, museum shows progression of American art over 150 years. Works by Robert Henri, George Luks, Grandma Moses, Norman Rockwell and Alfred Stieglitz, among others. Guided tours.

NATIONAL MODEL AVIATION MUSEUM – Muncie – 40 B6 Largest collection of modeling memorabilia and miniature aircraft in world. Exhibits trace nearly 100 years of model aviation, from fragile rubber band–powered relics to radio-controlled flyers and scale models.

NEEDMORE BUFFALO FARM – Elizabeth – 64 C3 500-acre working buffalo farm home to large North American bison herd. Buffalo burgers served at trading post. Guided wagon tours.

NORTHERN INDIANA CENTER FOR HISTORY – South Bend – 20 B6 10-acre historical museum complex. Voyages Gallery, History Center, Worker's Home Museum, children's museum and 38-room 1895–1896 mansion, Copshaholm. Gardens. Guided tours.

PERFECT NORTH SLOPES – Lawrenceburg – 53 B11 Ski resort with 16 runs and 400-foot vertical drop. 70 acres of tree-lined and open slopes. Four chairlifts; seven surface tows. Ski school. Equipment rentals.

CHILDREN'S ATTRACTIONS

CHILDREN'S MUSEUM – Indianapolis – 39 H8 One of world's largest children's museums. Exhibits (many interactive) on history, science and nature, world cultures and the arts. Large-format films shown in round theater. Historic hand-carved Dentzel carousel.

FT WAYNE CHILDREN'S ZOO – Ft Wayne – 29 C8 Houses over 1,000 animals from around world on 40 beautifully landscaped acres. Australian Adventure, Indonesian Rain Forest, African Veldt and Great Barrier Reef Aquarium. Endangered species carousel.

HOLIDAY WORLD & SPLASHIN' SAFARI – Santa Claus – 62 C5 Two parks in one offer more than 60 shows, games and rides, including wooden roller coaster "Raven," and trio of in-the-dark water slides. Wax and doll museums, petting zoo, Christmas area, live music.

INDIANA BEACH AMUSEMENT RESORT – Monticello – 25 H12 Park is home of "Hoosier Hurricane," state's first roller coaster. Water park with five water slides and action river. Also features sight-seeing paddle wheeler, the *Shafer Queen*. Adjacent campground.

INDIANAPOLIS ZOO – Indianapolis – 39 H7 64-acre zoo houses more than 3,000 species in regional habitats. Endangered Siberian tiger, lions, elephants, penguins and polar bears among animals represented. Aquarium. Dolphin shows.

MESKER PARK ZOO – Evansville – 61 E8 State's first and largest zoo contains over 700 animals from Africa, Asia, Australia, and South and North America. Train. Petting zoo. Paddle boats.

MUNCIE CHILDREN'S MUSEUM – Muncie – 40 B5 Museum contains Garfield exhibit based on feline cartoon-strip character created by local artist Jim Davis. Other exhibits include mock archaeological dig and model railroad. Guided tours.

SCIENCE CENTRAL – Ft Wayne – 29 C8 Interactive exhibits in math, science and technology. Visitors can walk on the moon, pick up live animals in a tidal pool or build a structure and see how it stands up to an earthquake.

REITZ HOME MUSEUM – Evansville – 61 E9 French Second Empire–style home, built 1871, features hand-laid wood parquet floors, stained glass windows and hand-painted ceilings. Period furnishings, many original to Reitz family. Guided tours.

RUTHMERE MUSEUM – Elkhart – 21 B10 1908–1910 house combines elaborate Beaux Arts–style with functional Prairie School–style architecture. Mahogany paneling, silk upholstered walls, painted ceilings and period furnishings. Underground tunnel connects to greenhouse. Guided tours.

SHELDON SWOPE ART MUSEUM – Terre Haute – 42 E5 Permanent and rotating exhibits of traditional and avant-garde works capture changing nature of American society. Artists include Thomas Hart Benton, Marc Chagall, Edward Hopper, Mary Fairchild MacMonnies and Andy Warhol.

STATE MUSEUM – Indianapolis – 39 H8 Museum of state's cultural and natural history housed in historic building. Exhibits on 30 years of Hoosier broadcast history, changing face of commerce and geologic past. Foucault pendulum. Guided tours.

WOLF PARK – Battle Ground – 31 D12 Education and research wildlife park features packs of wolves, herd of bison, coyotes and foxes. Guides explain social structure and role of wolves in wild. Guided tours.

Unique Natural Features

BLUESPRING CAVERNS – Bedford – 50 H3
Subterranean river and vaulted passages reveal wildlife adapted to perpetual darkness, such as crayfish, salamanders and beetles. Guided boat tours.

COWLES BOG – Indiana Dunes National Lakeshore – 19 C8 55-acre site combines marsh, bog and swamp characteristics. Rare stand of lady's slipper. Boardwalk. National Natural Landmark.

DEAM OAK – Bluffton – 29 H7 Extremely rare tree, discovered 1904, is hybrid of white and chinquapin oaks. Named for botanist C. C. Deam.

FALLS OF THE OHIO – Falls of the Ohio State Park – 58 H6 Approximately 1,000 acres of fossilized reefs contain over 400 species of coral. One of world's largest exposed Devonian fossil beds. Hiking. Picnic area. Interpretive center. National Natural Landmark.

HOOSIER PRAIRIE – Hoosier Prairie Nature Preserve – 18 D4 330-acre remnant prairie, once common in northwestern Indiana, supports rarely seen native plant species. Mainly cattail marsh and oak–prairie savanna. National Natural Landmark.

INDIANA DUNES – Dunes Nature Preserve – 19 B9 1,530-acre preserve extends almost 3 miles along shore of Lake Michigan. Exemplifies dunescape that once extended from Chicago, Illinois, area to Michigan. National Natural Landmark.

JUG ROCK – Jug Rock Nature Preserve – 56 B6 Oddly shaped standing rock. Slow process of erosion created pillar of sandstone, detached from main body of bedrock. Jug-like appearance.

KNOBSTONE ESCARPMENT – Clark State Forest – 58 D6 Prominent siltstone ridge stretches 150 miles from southern Johnson County across Ohio River to Kentucky. Marks easternmost section of Norman Upland region, exemplified by hills of Brown County.

LOST RIVER—ORANGEVILLE RISE – Orangeville Rise of Lost River Nature Preserve – 57 C9 Waters of partially subterranean Lost River "rise" at Orangeville at one of state's largest springs. National Natural Landmark.

LOST RIVER—WESLEY CHAPEL GULF – Orangeville – 57 C9 One of state's largest sinkholes (8.3-acre uvala formation) was formed by roof collapse in underground channel of Lost River. National Natural Landmark.

MARENGO CAVE – Marengo – 57 G11 Discovered in 1883, boasts more stalagmites than any other cave in state. Formations include war clubs, gypsum flowers and palettes. Guided tours. National Natural Landmark.

PINE HILLS – Pine Hills Nature Preserve – 37 F9 One of best examples of incised meanders (narrow, stream-carved rock ridges) in eastern US. Thriving species, considered Pleistocene-epoch relicts, include hemlock and Canada yew. National Natural Landmark.

PINHOOK BOG – Indiana Dunes National Lakeshore – 19 C11 One of few protected bogs in northern Indiana that occur in depressions of glacial origin. Illustrates ecological succession from pond to woodland. Tour reservations required. National Natural Landmark.

PORTLAND ARCH – Portland Arch Nature Preserve – 36 A5 Rare, 7.5-foot-high natural sandstone bridge cut by Bear Creek. Canyon climate supports plant species unknown elsewhere in state. National Natural Landmark.

ROCKY HOLLOW–FALLS CANYON – Rocky Hollow–Falls Canyon Nature Preserve – 37 G7 Steep sandstone canyons support virgin timber. Species include relict populations of eastern hemlock and Canada yew trees, in addition to some of Midwest's largest black walnut trees. National Natural Landmark.

TAMARACK BOG – Tamarack Bog Nature Preserve – 22 B6 Largest remaining tamarack swamp in state. Rare plants and animals, including lady's slipper, Indiana bat and starnose mole, occur on 100-acre site. National Natural Landmark.

WYANDOTTE CAVE – Harrison–Crawford/Wyandotte Complex – 63 A12 Cave encompasses greatest vertical relief of any cave in state and more than 23 miles of explored passageways. Visitor center. Guided tours. National Natural Landmark.

OLD-GROWTH FORESTS

DAVIS–PURDUE AGRICULTURAL CENTER FOREST – Brinckley – 41 A8 50-acre tract of near-virgin oak–hickory forest is among best examples in state. Exceptionally large trees include two burr oaks at 59 and 58 inches in diameter. National Natural Landmark.

DONALDSON CAVE/DONALDSONS WOODS – Donaldson Cave/Donaldsons Woods Nature Preserve – 57 A11 Much-studied caves represent Indiana karst region. Stream water flows from cave and winds along gorge bottom. Surrounding forest considered most impressive old-growth woods in state. National Natural Landmark.

E H BRYAN WOODS – Bryan Nature Preserve – 32 G3 Surrounded by farmland, 29-acre preserve characterized by tall, dense forest canopy. White oaks, 4 feet in diameter, share space with beech, hickory and basswood. Nature trail.

HEMMER WOODS – Hemmer Woods Nature Preserve – 61 A11 73 acres of old-growth forest part of what once covered southwestern Indiana.

Upland oak–hickory forest yields to southern-influenced bottomland of sweetgum, tulip and sycamore trees. National Natural Landmark.

PIONEER MOTHERS MEMORIAL FOREST – Hoosier National Forest – 57 D10 Protected for over 160 years, 88-acre site boasts one of state's best presettlement forests. Walnut grove contains trees measuring 60 feet to first limb and 3 feet in diameter. National Natural Landmark.

SHRADER–WEAVER WOODS – Shrader–Weaver Nature Preserve – 47 A7 28-acre site contains presettlement beech–maple forest and features one of highest concentrations of mature black walnut trees in US. Nature trails. National Natural Landmark.

WESSELMAN WOODS – Wesselman Woods Nature Preserve – 61 E9 One of state's finest presettlement lowland mixed forests covers 190 acres. Unusually high canopy and sweet gum–tulip tree domination. Nature center. Trails. National Natural Landmark.

Hiking

NAME, LOCATION	PAGE & GRID	LENGTH	TRAILHEAD	COMMENTS
Adventure Hiking Trail, Harrison–Crawford/Wyandotte Complex	63 B12	25-mile loop	Pioneer Cabin Shelter	Follows natural escarpments of Ohio and Blue rivers and Indian Creek. Rugged parts link with other Wyandotte Woods trails. Scenic overlooks. Moderate–Difficult.
Backcountry Loop, Jackson–Washington State Forest	58 A3	8-mile loop	Spurgeon Hollow Lake parking area	Rugged trail traverses densely forested area, passing scenic vistas, overlooks and ridge tops. Primitive camping. Difficult.
Bailly/Chellberg Trail, Indiana Dunes National Lakeshore	19 C8	2-mile loop	Bailly/Chellberg Visitor Center	Nature trail accesses many 19th-century historical structures, including Bailly Homestead and Chellberg Farm. Connects with Little Calumet River Trail. Bird-watching. Easy.
Chain O'Lakes State Park Trails, Burr Oak	22 G5	10-mile network	Park office	Trails traverse extensive park, passing beaches, wooded areas, swamps and open fields. Numerous river crossings. Includes self-guided nature trail. Easy–Moderate.
Clear Creek Rail–Trail, Bloomington	50 C3	4 miles	Clear Creek parking area	Dirt, gravel and original ballast trail meanders through southwest corner of city. Limestone walls create tunnel effect. Easy.
Dry Fork Loop, Clark State Forest	58 E5	12-mile network	Reed Road gravel parking area	Loops through primitive southwest corner of forest. Steep valleys, creek crossings and knobs. Trail network marked with color-coded posts. Difficult.
Forestry Management Trail, Selmier State Forest	52 D2	1-mile loop	Parking area	Self-guided tour through forest known for wildlife and timber management, watershed protection and outdoor recreation. Flat, gravel trail with few hills. Passes pond. Easy.
Fox Hollow Trail, Harrison–Crawford/Wyandotte Complex	63 B12	5 miles	North end of Horsemans Campground	Long descents and steep valleys make for scenic hike through wildlife habitat improvement area. Connects with Idlewild Trail. Multiuse. Moderate–Difficult.
Hickory Ridge Trails, Hoosier National Forest	50 E6	43-mile network	Hickory Ridge Horse Camp	Popular backwoods multiuse trail system provides steep hills and scenic valleys. Area characterized by remote, dense woodlands. Moderate–Difficult.
Indiana Dunes State Park Trails, Dune Acres	19 B9	16.5-mile network	Nature Center	Trails traverse park through dune, marsh and forest habitats. Diverse plant life; wildlife viewing. Examples of dune succession and scenic ridge-top lake views. Moderate.
Knobstone Trail, Clark State Forest	58 B5	58 miles	Leota Trailhead	Longest footpath in state traverses rugged bottomlands and steep ridge tops along rolling terrain. Wildlife viewing. Ends at Deam Lake Trailhead. Easy–Difficult.
Muscatatuck NWR Trails, Seymour	51 E12	11-mile network	Visitor center parking area	Roads link small loops and longer nature trails throughout wildlife refuge. Boardwalk crosses natural spring wetland. Deer, turkey and various waterfowl. Easy–Moderate.
Potato Creek State Park Trails, North Liberty	20 D5	14.5-mile network	Peppermint Hill Nature Center	Trail system spans vast park lands. Ridge-top views of lake give way to fields and winding forested paths. Nature center and observation deck. Easy–Difficult.
Prairie Duneland Trail, Portage	19 D7	6 miles	Countryside Park parking area	Asphalt multiuse rail–trail. When completed, will be 40-mile Lake Michigan Heritage Greenway. Easy.
Sand Ridge Trail, Tippecanoe River State Park	26 C2	2.5-mile loop	Fire tower parking area	Traverses sand hills and marsh area of unique natural area. Connects with extensive park trail system. Moderate.
Shades State Park Trails, Alamo	37 F9	10-mile network	Dell Shelter parking area	Challenging, marked trail system climbs steep ridges, ravines and streambeds. Skirts edge of Sugar Creek through Shawnee Canyon. Moderate–Difficult.
Shaw Loop, Clark State Forest	58 C6	5.5-mile loop	Richie Hollow Road trailhead	Great vistas along Shaw Lake characterize steep, rugged trail in far northeast corner of oldest designated state forest. Connects with Wildlife Loop. Moderate–Difficult.
Three Lakes Trail, Morgan–Monroe State Forest	44 H4	10-mile network	Forest office	Expansive loop connects Beanblossom, Bryant Creek and Cherry lakes. Rough terrain in parts. Traverses forest road, passing headquarters and lookout tower. Difficult.
Turkey Ridge Trail, Harrison–Crawford/Wyandotte Complex	63 B12	12 miles	West end of Horsemans Campground	Skirts Potato Run. Scenic overlooks of Indian Creek valley. Abundant wildlife viewing, including wild turkey, gray fox, deer and grouse. Moderate.
Wabash Heritage Trail, Battle Ground to Lafayette	31 E11	8 miles	Tippecanoe Battlefield	Scenic, flat footpath along Wabash River passes historical markers, parks and picnic areas. Bird-watching. Ends at Riehle Plaza. Easy.
West Beach Trail, Indiana Dunes National Lakeshore	19 C7	1-mile loop	West Beach Visitor Center	Interpretive trail excellent example of dune succession from bare sand beach through dune-building marram grass. Leads to oak forest. Steep-sided valleys. Easy.
Whitewater Memorial State Park Trails, Liberty	47 C10	11-mile network	Park road, south of saddle barn	Winding trail system through nature preserve and second-growth forest. Scenic overlooks. Skirts edge of Whitewater Lake. Easy–Difficult.

Biking

Most of the bicycle tours included in this chart are part of the Hoosier Bikeway System, administered by the Indiana Department of Natural Resources. These tours are mainly on less-traveled, secondary roads, and the routes for all are marked by signs.

NAME, LOCATION	PAGE & GRID	LENGTH	CLASS	COMMENTS
MOUNTAIN BIKING				
Bluhm Property Trails, Westville	19 D11	4.5-mile network	Moderate	Multiuse single-track trails traverse wetlands and forest. Switchbacks, short hills and some technical terrain. Wildflowers in spring.
Calumet Trail, Indiana Dunes National Lakeshore	19 C9	9.2 miles	Easy	Straight, flat corridor along edge of woods and prairie. Ends near Mt Baldy, 123-foot-high "live" dune. Off-road biking. Prairie Duneland Trail nearby.
France Park Trails, Logansport	32 A4	7-mile network	Easy–Difficult	Mostly single-track trails loop over varied terrain. Rocky, steep trail around limestone quarry begins above waterfall. Easier towpath along old canal. Fee.
Gnaw Bone Camp Trails, Gnaw Bone Camp	51 B7	25-mile network	Moderate	Network of 11 single-track trails occupy 1,560 acres. Hardwood forest and pasture. Hilly terrain offers some challenging technical climbs. Camp closed when trails are muddy. Fee.
Knobstone Trail, Elkinsville	51 D7	17 miles	Difficult	Single-track trail through lush, hilly hardwood forest follows ridge top above Middle Fork of Salt Creek. Surrounded by significant hills.
Tipsaw Trail, Tipsaw Lake Recreation Area	63 C8	7-mile loop	Easy–Moderate	Single-track gravel trail with a few challenging climbs in Hoosier National Forest. Scenery includes fields, forest and views of lake. Three rest stops.
Wapehani Mountain Bike Park, Bloomington	50 B3	7-mile network	Moderate	Network of single-track trails encircles lake over 35 wooded acres. Numerous short, steep hills and tight switchbacks. Only designated mountain biking park in state.
TOURING				
Hoosier Hills Route 1, Batesville to Clifty Falls SP	47 H7	61 miles	Moderate–Difficult	Travels south through Ripley and Jefferson counties. Accesses Versailles State Park after crossing covered bridge. Winds through hilly creek valley to town of Canaan.
Hoosier Hills Route 2, Clifty Falls SP to Brown County SP	52 H4	76 miles	Moderate	Extends west, accessing small towns and two recreation areas. Deep limestone ravines and waterfalls at Clifty Falls State Park. At mile 20, option to go right to Brown County State Park or left to Starve Hollow State Recreation Area.
Hoosier Hills Route 3, Starve Hollow SRA to St Meinrad	51 H8	88 miles	Moderate	Crosses East Fork of White River in Medora beside Medora Covered Bridge built in 1875. Accesses pioneer village and cave tours at Spring Mill State Park, town of French Lick and Patoka Lake.
Hoosier Hills Route 4, St Meinrad to Harmonie SP	62 B6	75 miles	Moderate	Scenic route travels west from St Meinrad, home to 1854 monastery, to town of New Harmony. Accesses town of Santa Claus, where post office receives millions of holiday letters. Side trip to Lincoln City.
Old National Road, Richmond to Indianapolis	41 H11	50 miles	Moderate	Mainly flat route along Old National Road, now US 40, east through Hancock, Henry and Wayne counties. Many 1800s historic sites. Madonna of the Trail, monument to pioneer women, at Glen Miller Park in Richmond.
Rivergreenway Recreational Trail, Ft Wayne	29 C8	12 miles	Easy	Multiuse urban trail along St Joseph and St Marys rivers. Starts at Johnny Appleseed Park and ends at Tillman Park. One of several river greenways—linear corridors for conservation—in state.
Sugar Creek Route, Indianapolis to Turkey Run State Park	38 G6	66 miles	Moderate	Begins at Eagle Creek Park and heads west. Scenic ride with few gentle hills. Stop at Shades State Park or continue 9 miles to Turkey Run State Park, both popular end points.
Taste of Honeyville Trail, Goshen to Honeyville	21 D12	21 miles	Easy–Moderate	Touring route through Amish community is blend of flat roads and rolling hills. Possible to continue to Shipshewana and Middlebury. One of four bike routes in Elkhart County area.
Wabash Valley Route 1, Shades State Park to West Lafayette	37 F9	59 miles	Moderate–Difficult	Route heads north on steep, winding road, crossing Deers Mill Covered Bridge just after 2 miles. Flattens out thereafter. Ends at Commandant's Home bed and breakfast.
Wabash Valley Route 2, West Lafayette to Mississinewa Lake Project	31 E11	75 miles	Moderate	Traverses Wabash River valley. Accesses Tippecanoe Battlefield National Historic Landmark and Wolf Park in Battle Ground; remnants of old Erie Canal in Delphi. Camping, picnicking and swimming at Mississinewa Lake.
Wabash Valley Route 3, Mississinewa Lake Project to Fox Island Co Park	33 B10	68 miles	Moderate	Level route travels northeast. Accesses six state parks and recreation areas, offering ample camping and picnicking opportunities.
Whitewater Valley Route, Richmond to Batesville	41 G12	71 miles	Moderate–Difficult	Rolls south along East Fork of Whitewater River to Whitewater Memorial State Park. Continues southwest to Batesville. Natural and historic attractions. Connects with Ohio's Cardinal Trail and Hoosier Hills Route 1.

Amish Country

AMISH ACRES – Nappanee – 21 F9 80-acre working farm and homestead of Stahly–Nissley–Kuhns family. Guided tours of 12-room white frame house, Switzer bank barn and 18 additional outbuildings. Craft demonstrations.

AMISHVILLE USA – Berne – 35 C10 Restored Amish farmhouse and outbuildings in rural setting. 1800s working gristmill. Horse-drawn buggy rides. Camping. Guided tours.

ELKHART – Elkhart – 21 A10 Festivals, farmers' market, local art, antique auto museum, railroad museum and Midwest Museum of American Art. Beaux arts/Prairie School–style Ruthmere Museum built 1908.

GASTHOF AMISH VILLAGE – Montgomery – 56 B3 Theme village encompasses market, furniture shop, and craft shows and demonstrations. Restaurant in historic barn created by Amish carpenters. Flea market. Festivals. Horse-drawn buggy tours of area.

GOSHEN – Goshen – 21 C12 Horse-drawn buggies provide transportation to annual Elkhart County 4-H Fair. Old Bag Factory shops housed in 1895 Cosmo Buttermilk Soap company building. Renovated with original beams and floors.

HERITAGE TRAIL – Elkhart – 21 A10 Self-guided audio tour of several key Amish towns. 90-mile loop reveals characteristic sights: horse-drawn buggies, round barns and farms that forgo use of power equipment. Elkhart to Shipshewana to Nappanee. Tapes available at Elkhart Visitors Center.

MENNO-HOF – Shipshewana – 22 B3 Museum's interactive displays show origins and culture of Amish and Mennonite communities. Various exhibits include sailing ship replica, cobblestone street, meetinghouse, dungeon. Rough-hewn barn. Guided tours.

MIDDLEBURY – Middlebury – 22 B1 Family-owned Amish Heritage Furniture features original pieces from mid-1800s. Country inns, crafts and antiques. Classic automobiles. Annual festivals.

MONTGOMERY – Montgomery – 56 B3 Crafts, quilts, barns, buggy shop, furniture, active one-room schoolhouse. Dillon Amish Country Tours include dinner and visits to Amish homes, craft shops and country stores.

NAPPANEE – Nappanee – 21 F9 Antiques auctions, furniture, quilt shops, annual festivals. Old-fashioned marketplace Borkholder Dutch Village displays local crafts and household goods.

ROUND BARN THEATER – Nappanee – 21 F9 Restored 1911 round barn part of Amish Acres farm complex. Amish-themed musicals performed by professional cast. Proscenium stage. 400 seats.

SHIPSHEWANA – Shipshewana – 22 B3 Riegsecker Marketplace, horse-drawn buggy rides, shops, quilts, furniture, crafts and antiques. One of largest ongoing outdoor flea markets in Midwest hosts 1,000 vendors.

WAKARUSA – Wakarusa – 21 D9 Amish-style restaurant, shops, antique tractor collection and Wakarusa Historical Society. Train rides on Old Wakarusa Railroad; main engine built 1957, modeled after 1862 General Locomotive.

Scenic Drives

COVERED BRIDGE DRIVING TOUR – Rockville – 38-mile loop – 43 A7 Rustic roads traverse farmland and access six covered bridges, including 1856 Crooks Bridge, county's oldest. Bridgeton Mill, bridge and waterfall. Five possible routes start and end at Parke County Visitor Center. ROUTE: CR 80E, CR 320E, CR 150E, CR 890E, CR 850E, CR 40E, CR 550W, US 41.

HERITAGE TRAIL – Elkhart – 90-mile loop – 21 A10 Tour through picturesque towns and rolling farmland of Amish country. Many points of interest. Audiotapes and guidebook available at Elkhart Visitors Center. ROUTE: SR 19, CR 52, CR 101, US 6, CR 7, SR 119, CR 22, US 20, CR 1000W, CR 400S, SR 5, CR 16, CR 8, SR 120.

LIGHTHOUSES, LAKES AND LANES – Michigan City – 120-mile loop – 19 A12 Self-guided tour of northern Indiana harbor country highlights historical and cultural heritage of LaPorte County. Starts and ends at LaPorte County Visitor Center. ROUTE: Meer Road, US 35, US 421, US 30, SR 39, CR 800S, CR 400W, US 6, Wozniak Road, SR 2, CR 400E, CR 500E, CR 1000N, US 12, Meer Road.

LINCOLN HERITAGE TRAIL – New Albany to Vincennes – 132 miles – 58 H6 Winding route along two-lane roads traces life of revered president across Kentucky, Indiana and Illinois. Family homestead where Lincoln grew up is among historic sites in Indiana. ROUTE: (Indiana only) SR 64, SR 37, SR 62, SR 162, US 231, SR 56, SR 61.

MUSCATATUCK NATIONAL WILDLIFE REFUGE AUTO TOUR – Seymour – 3-mile loop – 51 E12 Interpretive tour on gravel road explains wetland ecology. Marsh, farmland, grassland and green-tree reservoirs—shallow water resting and feeding areas for ducks and other waterfowl. ROUTE: Gravel road starts and ends near wildlife refuge visitor center.

OHIO RIVER SCENIC ROUTE – Lawrenceburg to Mt Vernon – 303 miles – 53 C11 Designated National Scenic Byway along Ohio River through agricultural landscape, forest and small towns. Natural and historic sites, scenic overlooks. ROUTE: SR 56, SR 156, SR 56, SR 62, SR 66, US 164, SR 62.

OLD NATIONAL ROAD – Richmond to Indianapolis – 50 miles – 41 H11 Tour along route, now US 40 but nicknamed "Antique Alley," that served as 1800s thoroughfare of trade, culture and migration. Historic structures from National Road era. Antique shops. ROUTE: US 40.

PERRY COUNTY AUTO TOUR – Cannelton – 80-mile loop – 63 F7 Tour through eastern half of county begins in historic Cannelton. Accesses several towns and historic sites. Rolling hills. Black arrows marking route begin in Tobinsport. ROUTE: SR 66, SR 166, CR 1, SR 66, CR 27, SR 182, SR 66, CR 34, SR 37, CR 70, CR 21, CR 10, CR 5, SR 66.

To locate fishing spots in this Atlas, look on the given page for the fishing symbol and corresponding four-digit number. It is important to be familiar with all rules, regulations and restrictions before fishing in any area. For licensing information and a guidebook to fishing in Indiana, contact the Indiana Department of Natural Resources, Division of Fish and Wildlife, in Indianapolis. Lakes of fewer than 75 acres were not included in this chart.

NUMBER, BODY OF WATER	PAGE & GRID	ACREAGE	LARGEMOUTH BASS	SMALLMOUTH BASS	HYBRID STRIPED BASS	STRIPED BASS	BLUEGILL/REDEAR	CARP	CATFISH	CRAPPIE	MUSKELLUNGE	YELLOW PERCH	NORTHERN PIKE	SALMON	SAUGER	TROUT	WALLEYE
3000 Adams Lake	22 D6	303	•	•			•			•							
3004 Anderson River	62 E6	—		•		•							•	•			
3008 Atwood Lake	22 D5	170	•	•			•										
3010 Augusta Lake	56 G1	110		•			•	•									•
3012 Ball Lake	23 D10	87	•	•													
3016 Bass Lake	26 A3	1,345	•	•				•									•
3020 Bear Lake	22 H3	136	•				•										
3024 Beaver Dam Lake	27 C10	146	•	•			•		•								
3028 Beaver Dam Lake	56 F5	205	•	•			•										
3032 Big Blue River	46 B1	—					•							•			
3036 Big Chapman Lake	21 H12	512	•				•										
3040 Big Lake	22 H3	228	•				•										
3044 Big Long Lake	23 D7	365	•				•		•								
3048 Big Raccoon Creek	43 A9	—												•			
3052 Big Turkey Lake	23 C7	450	•				•										
3056 Bischoff Reservoir	47 H7	190	•	•			•		•	•							
3060 Black Oak Bayou	24 B4	—	•	•	•			•		•							
3064 Blue Lake	28 A5	239	•	•			•										
3068 Blue River	63 B12	—	•	•	•		•	•		•		•					
3072 Brookville Lake	47 E10	5,260	•	•	•	•	•	•	•	•	•						•
3076 Bruce Lake	26 D4	245	•	•			•										
3080 Brush Creek Reservoir	52 D3	167	•	•			•		•	•							
3084 Carr Lake	27 B11	79	•	•			•		•								
3088 Cass Lake	22 B2	89	•	•			•										
3092 Cecil M Harden Lake	43 A9	2,060	•	•	•		•	•	•	•							
3096 Cedar Lake	22 A5	120	•				•	•									
3100 Cedar Lake	28 A4	131	•	•			•							•			
3104 Cedar Lake	18 G4	781			•	•		•		•							
3108 Cedarville Reservoir	29 B9	245	•					•	•								
3112 Center Lake	27 A11	140	•						•								
3116 Clear Lake	23 A11	800	•				•								•		•
3120 Clear Lake	20 C1	106	•						•								
3124 Clock Creek	22 E5	—												•			
3128 Cobus Creek	21 B9	—												•			
3132 Cree Lake	22 E6	76	•		•		•										
3136 Crooked Creek	19 F10	—												•			
3140 Crooked Lake	28 A4	206	•	•			•										
3144 Crooked Lake	23 B9	800	•	•			•										
3148 Dewart Lake	21 G12	551	•	•			•										
3152 Diamond Lake	22 F3	105	•				•										
3156 Dogwood Lake	56 D3	1,400	•				•		•	•	•						
3160 Driftwood River	51 B10	—	•				•		•								
3164 Eagle Creek Reservoir	38 G6	1,350	•	•			•	•	•	•							
3168 Eagle Lake	22 F3	81	•				•										
3172 East Fork of White River	50 H3	—	•	•				•	•	•				•			
3176 Eel River	27 G9	—		•		•			•								
3180 Elkhart River	22 E1	—		•		•			•								
3184 Fawn River	23 A7	—													•		
3188 Fish Lake	20 D3	275	•	•			•			•				•			
3192 Fish Lake	22 C6	145	•	•			•										
3196 Flat Rock River	46 G1	—		•			•		•								
3200 Fox Lake	23 C9	142	•	•			•		•								
3204 Glenn Flint Lake	43 A10	371	•	•			•		•								
3208 Golden Lake	23 C9	119	•	•			•										
3212 Grassy Creek Chain of Lakes	22 H1	1,133	•				•										
3216 Hamilton Lake	23 D10	802	•	•			•			•							
3220 Hardy Lake	52 H1	745	•	•			•		•	•							
3224 Hovey Lake	60 H4	1,400	•	•			•		•	•							
3228 Huntingburg Lake	56 H4	188	•	•				•	•								
3232 Huntington Lake	28 G4	900	•	•			•	•	•	•							
3236 Hurshtown Reservoir	29 A10	260	•		•		•										
3240 Iroquois River	25 F8	—		•	•				•	•			•				
3244 J C Murphy Lake	24 E3	1,000	•	•			•		•	•			•				
3248 Jackson Creek	50 B5	—												•			
3252 Kankakee River	19 H12	—	•	•			•		•	•							
3256 Knapp Lake	22 G2	120	•				•		•								
3260 Kokomo Reservoir	33 E9	482	•	•			•		•	•							
3264 Koontz Lake	20 F4	346	•	•			•										
3268 Kuhn Lake	22 H1	850	•				•										
3272 Lake Celina	63 B8	164	•	•			•										
3276 Lake Freeman	31 B12	1,547	•	•			•		•	•							
3280 Lake Gage	23 B8	327	•	•			•										
3284 Lake George	23 A9	509	•	•			•		•		•						
3288 Lake James	23 B9	1,039	•	•			•			•	•						
3292 Lake Lemon	50 A5	1,440	•	•			•		•								
3296 Lake Manitou	27 D7	731	•	•			•		•	•			•				

NUMBER, BODY OF WATER	PAGE & GRID	ACREAGE	LARGEMOUTH BASS	SMALLMOUTH BASS	HYBRID STRIPED BASS	STRIPED BASS	BLUEGILL/REDEAR	CARP	CATFISH	CRAPPIE	MUSKELLUNGE	YELLOW PERCH	NORTHERN PIKE	SALMON	SAUGER	TROUT	WALLEYE
3300 Lake Maxinkukee	26 B5	1,854	•	•	•		•			•	•						•
3304 Lake Michigan	18 B6	—											•	•	•	•	
3308 Lake Michigan	19 C8	—					•									•	
3312 Lake of the Woods	21 F7	416	•	•			•		•	•							
3316 Lake of the Woods	23 D7	136	•	•			•										
3320 Lake Sullivan	48 C5	461	•	•			•		•	•							
3324 Lake Waveland	37 G8	358	•				•		•	•	•						
3328 Lake Wawasee	22 F1	3,410	•	•	•		•										•
3332 Laughery Creek	53 E10	—		•					•					•	•		
3336 Little Chapman Lake	21 H12	177	•				•										•
3340 Little Elkhart River	22 B1	—		•					•								
3344 Little Turkey Lake	23 C7	124	•	•			•		•								
3348 Loon Lake	23 B9	138	•	•			•			•	•						
3352 Loon Lake	22 H3	222	•				•										
3356 Middlefork Lake	41 G11	177	•	•			•										
3360 Mill Creek	27 C7	—							•								
3364 Mill Pond Lake	20 H5	168	•				•		•								
3368 Mississinewa Lake	33 A10	3,280	•	•			•		•	•	•						•
3372 Monroe Lake	50 D4	10,750	•	•	•		•	•	•	•	•						•
3376 Muscatatuck River	51 H8	—		•			•		•								
3380 Nyona Lake	27 E7	104	•				•		•								
3384 Ohio River	63 C11	—		•					•	•							
3388 Olin Lake	22 D5	103	•				•										•
3392 Oliver Lake	22 D5	500	•	•			•										
3396 Otter Lake	23 C7	190	•	•			•		•								
3400 Palestine Lake	27 B10	290	•	•			•		•								
3404 Patoka Lake	57 F7	8,880	•	•			•		•	•	•						
3408 Patoka River	56 G4	—		•					•	•							
3412 Pigeon Creek	23 B7	—							•						•		
3416 Pigeon River	22 B5	—		•					•						•		
3420 Pine Lake	20 C1	564	•				•		•								
3424 Pleasant Lake	20 E6	106	•	•			•		•								
3428 Potato Creek	20 D4	—					•									•	
3432 Pretty Lake	23 D7	185	•	•			•			•			•			•	
3436 Prides Creek Lake	55 E12	90	•				•		•	•							
3440 Rockville Lake	37 H7	100	•				•		•	•							
3444 Round Lake	28 A4	131	•	•			•										•
3448 Rowe–Eden Ditch	22 C2	—															•
3452 Salamonie Lake	28 H2	1,260	•				•		•	•							
3456 Sechrist Lake	22 H1	99					•		•								
3460 Shipshewana Lake	22 B2	202	•				•		•								
3464 Shriner Lake	28 A4	120	•				•			•			•				
3468 Simonton Lake	21 A10	299	•	•			•										
3472 Skinner Lake	22 F5	125	•				•		•		•	•					
3476 Solomon Creek	21 E12	—														•	
3480 South Mud Lake	27 F7	94	•				•		•								
3484 South Twin Lake	22 A4	116	•				•										•
3488 Spy Run Creek	29 C8	—														•	
3492 St Joseph River	29 C8	—	•	•					•				•	•			
3496 St Joseph River	21 B7	—		•					•								
3500 Starve Hollow Lake	51 H9	145	•				•		•	•							
3504 Stone Lake	20 C1	564		•													
3508 Story Lake	23 E8	77	•				•										
3512 Sugar Creek	37 F8	—		•					•		•	•					
3520 Summit Lake	40 D6	600	•	•			•		•	•	•						
3524 Syracuse Lake	22 F1	414	•	•			•		•								
3528 Tippecanoe River	31 B12	—		•	•		•		•								•
3532 Tipsaw Lake	63 C8	131	•				•		•	•							
3536 Trail Creek	19 B11	—												•	•	•	
3540 Turkey Creek	22 B6	—							•							•	
3544 Turtle Creek Lake	48 D3	1,550	•	•			•		•	•							•
3548 Vernon Fork of Muscatatuck River	52 E2	—							•								
3552 Versailles Lake	53 C7	230	•				•		•	•							
3556 Wabash River	32 B3	—		•					•	•							
3560 Wall Lake	23 A7	141	•	•			•										•
3564 Webster Lake	22 G1	744	•	•			•		•	•	•		•				
3568 West Lakes	22 E4	454	•	•			•		•		•	•					
3572 Westwood Lake	40 F4	173	•	•			•		•								
3576 White River	39 D9	—		•					•	•							
3580 Wildcat Creek	32 E3	—		•					•								
3584 Winona Lake	27 A12	562	•	•			•										•
3588 Witmer Lake	22 D5	685	•				•										
3592 Wolf Lake	18 B3	385	•		•		•										
3596 Worster Lake	20 D5	327	•	•			•		•	•							
3600 Yellow River	20 H2	—		•					•								
3604 Yellowwood Lake	50 B5	133	•	•			•		•								

Hunting

For licensing information and a guidebook to hunting in Indiana, contact the Indiana Department of Natural Resources, Division of Fish and Wildlife, in Indianapolis. Hunting areas of fewer than 100 acres were not included in this chart.

NAME, LOCATION	PAGE & GRID	ACREAGE	Mandatory Check In	Shooting Range / Archery Range	Camping	Coyote	Deer	Dove	Fox	Grouse	Opossum	Pheasant	Quail	Rabbit	Raccoon	Snipe	Squirrel	Turkey	Waterfowl	Woodcock
Atterbury Fish and Wildlife Area	45 G9	6,029	●	●		●	●	●	●		●	●	●	●	●		●	●		
Barnes–Seng Wetland Conservation Area	56 G4	105					●												●	
Brookville Lake Project	47 E10	16,445	●	●	●	●	●			●	●		●	●	●		●	●	●	●
Brush Creek Fish and Wildlife Area	52 D3	1,841				●	●	●	●		●		●	●	●		●	●		
Cagles Mill Lake Project	43 E11	8,780				●	●	●			●		●	●	●		●	●		
Camp Atterbury Maneuver Training Center	45 G9	35,000				●			●											
Cedar Swamp Wetland Conservation Area	23 A11	863					●				●				●				●	
Clark State Forest	58 D6	24,500	●	●			●	●												
Crosley Fish and Wildlife Area	52 E2	4,181	●	●		●	●	●	●		●		●	●	●		●	●		
Deniston Resource Area	28 A2	300				●	●							●						
Eagle Lake Wetland Conservation Area	22 F3	137					●				●				●					
Ferdinand State Forest	63 A7	7,640				●	●													
Ferdinand State Forest—Pike Unit	56 G2	2,814				●	●													
Fish Lake Wetland Conservation Area	20 D3	240					●	●												
Galena Wetland Conservation Area	20 B1	165					●	●												
Glendale Fish and Wildlife Area	56 D3	8,061				●	●	●	●		●		●	●	●		●	●		
Greene–Sullivan State Forest	48 D6	7,964	●				●				●				●					
Hardy Lake State Recreation Area	52 H1	2,120	●				●				●				●					
Harrison–Crawford/Wyandotte Complex	63 B12	25,349				●	●	●			●			●	●		●	●		
Hillenbrand Fish and Wildlife Area	49 C7	3,200				●	●	●	●		●		●	●	●		●	●		
Hoosier National Forest	63 F8	192,000				●	●				●				●		●	●		
Hovey Lake Fish and Wildlife Area	60 H4	4,425				●	●				●			●	●		●	●		
Huntington State Recreation Area	28 G4	8,217	●	●		●	●	●	●		●	●	●	●	●		●	●		
Jackson–Washington State Forest	51 G9	15,600				●	●	●			●			●	●		●	●		
Jasper–Pulaski Fish and Wildlife Area	25 C10	8,000	●	●		●	●	●	●		●	●	●	●	●		●	●	●	
Kankakee River Fish and Wildlife Area	20 H1	4,095	●			●	●				●	●	●	●	●		●	●	●	
Kingsbury Fish and Wildlife Area	20 D2	5,062	●	●		●	●	●	●		●	●	●	●	●		●	●	●	
LaSalle Fish and Wildlife Area	24 B4	3,643				●	●				●		●	●	●		●	●	●	

NAME, LOCATION	PAGE & GRID	ACREAGE	Mandatory Check In	Shooting Range / Archery Range	Camping	Coyote	Deer	Dove	Fox	Grouse	Opossum	Pheasant	Quail	Rabbit	Raccoon	Snipe	Squirrel	Turkey	Waterfowl	Woodcock
Little Pigeon Creek Wetland Conservation Area	62 C3	846					●				●			●	●		●			
Mallard Roost Wetland Conservation Area	22 E3	760					●				●				●				●	
Manitou Islands Wetland Conservation Area and Nature Preserve	27 D7	129					●													
Marsh Lake Wetland Conservation Area	23 A10	800					●	●	●		●				●				●	
Martin State Forest	57 B7	7,023				●	●				●				●		●	●		
Menominee Wetland Conservation Area	20 H5	830					●				●				●				●	
Minnehaha Fish and Wildlife Area	48 C5	11,400	●	●		●	●	●			●			●	●		●	●		
Mississinewa Lake Project	33 B10	14,386				●	●	●			●			●	●		●	●		
Modoc Wildlife Management Area	41 D9	166					●				●				●					
Monroe Lake Project	50 C4	23,952	●	●		●	●	●			●			●	●		●	●		
Morgan–Monroe State Forest	44 H4	23,555				●	●				●				●		●	●		
Muscatatuck National Wildlife Refuge	51 E12	7,724					●				●			●	●		●	●	●	
Owen–Putnam State Forest	43 H11	6,193				●	●				●				●		●	●		
Patoka Lake Project	57 F7	25,583				●	●				●			●	●		●	●		
Pigeon River Fish and Wildlife Area	22 B6	11,600	●			●	●				●	●	●	●	●		●	●	●	
Raccoon State Recreation Area	43 A9	4,065	●			●	●				●			●	●		●	●		
Round Lake Wetland Conservation Area and Nature Preserve	26 A2	140					●													
Salamonie Lake Project	34 A2	11,056				●	●	●			●			●	●		●	●		
Selmier State Forest	52 D2	355					●				●				●		●			
Splinter Ridge Fish and Wildlife Area	59 G10	2,491				●	●				●			●	●		●	●		
Sugar Ridge Fish and Wildlife Area	56 G1	7,300	●	●		●	●	●			●			●	●		●	●		
Tri-County Fish and Wildlife Area	22 G1	3,486	●	●		●	●	●	●		●	●	●	●	●		●	●	●	
Wilbur Wright Fish and Wildlife Area	40 E5	1,200	●	●		●	●	●	●		●	●	●	●	●		●	●		
Willow Slough Fish and Wildlife Area	24 E3	9,909	●	●		●	●	●	●		●	●	●	●	●		●	●	●	
Winamac Fish and Wildlife Area	26 C2	4,650	●	●		●	●	●	●		●	●	●	●	●		●	●	●	
Yellowwood State Forest	50 B5	22,451				●	●				●				●		●	●		

Campgrounds

To locate these campgrounds in this Atlas, look on the given page for the campground symbol and corresponding four-digit number.

NUMBER, NAME, LOCATION	PAGE & GRID	RV SITES	TENTING
4000 Add-More Campground, Cementville	58 G6	60	
4010 Amishville USA Campground, Geneva	35 C10	300	●
4020 Beaver Ridge Family Camping, Lakeville	20 D6	138	●
4030 Blackhawk Campground, Cloverdale	43 E11	158	●
4040 Candy Stripe Campsite, Lake Eliza	19 F8	92	●
4050 Circle B Park, Angola	23 C8	250	●
4060 Cloverdale RV Park, Cloverdale	43 D12	72	●
4070 Columbus Woods-n-Waters, Ogilville	51 C10	102	●
4080 Crawfordsville KOA, Crawfordsville	37 D11	60	●
4090 Deer Ridge Camping Resort, Richmond	41 G11	64	●
4100 Donna-Jo Camping Area, Kouts	25 A10	60	●
4110 Driftwood Camp and RV Park, Taylorsville	45 H10	60	
4120 E Z Kamp, Grovertown	20 G3	107	
4130 Eby's Pines, Bristol	22 A1	330	●
4140 Elkhart Campground, Elkhart	21 A10	450	●
4150 Elkhart County/Middlebury Exit KOA, Middlebury	22 A1	105	●
4160 Fairland Recreation Park, Fairland	45 C12	48	●
4170 GloWood Campground, Pendleton	39 E11	50	●
4180 Golden Rule Campground, Winchester	41 B9	78	●
4190 Gordon's Camping, Woodruff	23 D7	750	●
4200 Grandpa's Farm, Middleboro	41 G11	75	●
4210 Hickory Grove Lakes Campground, New Pittsburg	35 H10	98	●
4220 Hidden Lake Campground, Fairmount	33 G12	125	●
4230 Hoffman Lake Camp, Warsaw	21 H10	50	●
4240 Honey Bear Hollow Family Campground, Peru	27 H8	100	●
4250 Hoosier Hideaway, Kewanna	26 D4	70	
4260 Indian Lakes Resort, Morris	47 H8	1,200	●
4270 Indian Springs Campground, Butler Center	23 H8	350	●
4280 Indiana Beach Camp Resort, Monticello	25 H12	856	●
4290 Indiana–Ohio KOA, Richmond	41 G11	50	●
4300 Kamp Modoc, Modoc	41 D8	250	●
4310 Kamper Korner, Indianapolis	45 B7	100	●
4320 KOA Indianapolis, Greenfield	39 H11	195	●
4330 Lafayette AOK Kampground, Lafayette	31 G11	160	●
4340 Lake in the Pines Campground, Sunman	53 A9	150	●
4350 Lake Monroe Village, Smithville	50 D4	125	●
4360 Lake Rudolph Outdoor Resort, Santa Claus	62 C4	90	●
4370 Lakeview Campground, Rochester	27 C8	103	●
4380 Last Resort Campground, Hanna	19 F12	81	●
4390 Last Resort RV Park & Campground, Nashville	51 B7	143	●
4400 Louisville Metro KOA, Jeffersonville	58 H6	97	●
4410 Manapogo Park, Orland	23 A8	60	●
4420 Mar-Brook Campground, Gas City	34 E3	230	●
4430 Menefee's Camp Sack-In, Metz	23 B12	30	●
4440 Michigan City Campground, Michigan City	19 C11	100	●
4450 Mini Mountain Campground, New Carlisle	20 B4	184	●
4460 Moccasin Meadow Campground, Clarksburg	46 F6	24	●
4470 New Lisbon Campground, New Lisbon	41 G7	124	●
4480 Oak Lake Family Campground, Roselawn	24 C6	250	●
4490 Old Mill Run Park, Thorntown	38 C2	400	●
4500 Patona Bay Resort, Oswego	21 G12	8	●
4510 Raceview Family Campground, Brownsburg	38 H5	100	●
4520 Riverside Campground, Shipshewana	22 A3	30	●
4530 Rupert's Resort Campground, Bremen	21 F7	20	●
4540 S & H Campground, Greenfield	39 H11	125	●
4550 Scenic Campground, Brookville	47 F10	60	●
4560 Scenic Hills Campground, Middlebury	22 A1	96	●
4570 Shipshewana Campground, Shipshewana	22 B3	72	●
4580 Shipshewana Campground & Amish Log Cabin Lodging, Shipshewana	22 A2	45	●
4590 South Bend East KOA, Granger	21 A8	50	●
4600 Sports Lake Campground, Washington	34 E3	157	●
4610 State Fairgrounds, Indianapolis	39 G8	172	●
4620 Sugar Creek Campground, Thorntown	38 C3	103	●
4630 Summers Campground, Attica	30 F6	30	●
4640 Tall Sycamore Campground, Logansport	32 A6	15	●
4650 Terre Haute KOA, Terre Haute	42 F6	78	●
4660 Twin Mills Resort, Howe	22 A4	520	●
4670 Walnut Ridge Resort Campground, New Castle	40 F4	180	●
4680 Westward Ho Campground, Gnaw Bone	51 B8	115	●
4690 Yogi Bear's Jellystone Park Camp Resort, Pierceton	28 A1	150	●
4700 Yogi Bear's Jellystone Park Camp Resort, Knightstown	40 G3	135	●
4710 Yogi Bear's Jellystone Park Camp Resort, Plymouth	20 G5	1,096	●
4720 Yogi Bear's Jellystone Park— Barton Lake, Jamestown	23 A9	250	●
4730 Yogi Bear's Jellystone Park— Lake Holiday, Roselawn	24 B6	674	●
4740 Yogi Bear's Jellystone Park— Raintree Lake, Little York	58 B5	71	●

Canoe Trips

NAME, TOWN/ROUTE	PAGE & GRID	LENGTH (miles)	PUT-IN	TAKEOUT	COMMENTS
Big Pine Creek, Rainsville to Attica	30 F6	14.5	Access site	Quabache Park	Clear creek best run in spring. Offers natural beauty and challenging whitewater section. Sharp turns, chutes and standing waves. Sandstone ledges. Novices should avoid Rocky Ford area near Rainsville.
Big Walnut Creek, North Salem to Greencastle	38 G1	24.6	CR 900 bridge	Grenel Road bridge southwest of town	Stream with few riffles suitable for novices and intermediates. Flows through deep valley with rare plant species, past farmland and under four covered bridges.
Blue River, Fredericksburg to Harrison–Crawford/Wyandotte Complex	58 F1	47	US 150 bridge	Stagestop Campground	River with gradient of 4 feet per mile flows between limestone walls blanketed with trees and shrubs. Caves and sinkholes. Portages at three dams.
Deep River, Merrillville to Hobart	19 E7	6	Deep River County Park bridge	Arizona Street bridge southwest of town	Slow, muddy river. Densely wooded banks provide natural oasis amidst heavily used agricultural and residential lands. Logjams possible.
Driftwood River, Edinburgh to Columbus	45 G10	16	Camp Atterbury Road bridge	Mill Race Park	River formed by confluence of Big Blue River and Sugar Creek winds through farmland. Forested banks with some development at southern end.
East Fork of White River, Columbus to Williams	51 B10	189	Access site at old railroad depot	South of dam off SR 450	Slow stream through forest, rocky terrain and farmland. Sandbars and picturesque islands. Two series of rapids below Hindostan Falls. Camping.
East Race Waterway, South Bend	21 B7	0.38	Niles Avenue at Jefferson Boulevard	Niles Avenue at Madison Street	Shunt off St Joseph River is first artificial whitewater course in North America and one of six in world. Public inner tubing, rafting and kayaking in summer.
Eel River, Laketon to Logansport	27 E11	50	Access site	Spencer Park	Quiet, scenic river with tree-lined banks and bordering farms. Slow float picks up in last 28-mile, boulder-bottomed stretch known for stream fishing. Dams.
Elkhart River, Millersburg to Elkhart	22 E1	31.2	SR 13 bridge	Island Park	Slow-moving river through area of farms, woods and marshland. Logjams and heavy aquatic vegetation in upper reaches. Dam portages. Camping at Oxbow Park.
Fawn River, Howe to Orland	22 A4	33	CR 700N bridge	CR 600W bridge	River follows narrow, twisting corridor lined with willow, elm and hickory trees; marsh area as well. Takeout at Greenfield Mills Pond for 10-mile day trip.
Flatrock River, Geneva to Columbus	45 F12	23	SR 9 bridge	US 31 bridge	Section of river once lined with mills provides trip of moderate difficulty. Willows on gravel bars; wooded banks. Steep access. Two dam portages.
Iroquois River, Brook to Kentland	24 G6	16	SR 16 bridge	State line bridge	Shallow, slow-moving muddy river through prairie and woodland. Banks pocketed with swamp milkweed and rose mallow, oak, hickory, walnut, willow and ash trees. Ends at Illinois state line.
Kankakee River, Kingsford Heights to Demotte	20 E3	48	Kingsbury Fish and Wildlife Area	CR 600 bridge (east of I-65)	Wetlands along river rich with wildlife, including rare species: greater prairie chicken, sandhill crane, osprey, and golden and bald eagles. Camping at Kingsbury and Kankakee River fish and wildlife areas.
Mississinewa River, Albany to Gas City	34 H6	26	SR 28 bridge	Gas City Park	Slow-moving section of rock-bottomed river that flows through flat, wide valley. Corridor lined with sycamore and cottonwood. Two portages.
North Fork of Wildcat Creek, Cutler to Lafayette	32 E3	36	Adams Mill public fishing area	Davis Ferry County Park	Scenic river passes under Lancaster Covered Bridge. Reliable water level with gravel bars and riffles. Flow doubles after confluence with South Fork of Wildcat Creek.
Pigeon River, Mongo to Scott	22 B6	20.5	CR 900E bridge	CR 750N bridge	River hugs face of moraine for much of length. Abundant wildlife. Midpoint takeout at SR 9 bridge. Three portages. Camping at Pigeon River Fish and Wildlife Area.
South Branch of Elkhart River, Albion to Wawaka	22 G4	11.75	River Road bridge	US 6 bridge	Lazy river meanders by wooded nature preserve and extensive wetlands, including Mallard Roost Wetland Conservation Area. Migratory waterfowl.
South Fork of Wildcat Creek, Lafayette	31 F12	13	SR 26 access site	Davis Ferry County Park	Creek best run in spring flows through flat farmland fringed with trees. Several glacial kames (mounds) visible. Access at mile 4 at confluence with North Fork of Wildcat Creek.
St Joseph River, Bristol to South Bend	21 A12	19.5	SR 15 access site	Access site 0.5 mile south of I-80/90 bridge	Begins in farmland; takes on urban flavor as it flows to Elkhart, Mishawaka and South Bend. Strenuous portage around dam at mile 10. Access to East Race Waterway in South Bend.
St Joseph River, Newville to Ft Wayne	23 G11	40	SR 8 bridge	Access site south of SR 930 bridge	Wide, slow stream through hardwood forest and farmland. First 17 miles to Spencerville dam access most secluded section. Two portages. Possible logjams. Camping at Johnny Appleseed Memorial Park.
Sugar Creek, Crawfordsville to West Union	37 D11	39	Elston Park	West Union Bridge	Named for sugar maple trees lining banks, clear stream considered one of state's most scenic. Mainly riffles and pools, but can be dangerous in high water. Cliffs, bluffs and three covered bridges.
Tippecanoe River, Etna Green to Tippecanoe River State Park	27 A9	57	Mollenhour access site	Access site	Scenic river bordered by green fields and forest of maple, sycamore and willow. Small islands and high bluffs add to beauty. Numerous access points. Camping.
Tippecanoe River, Springboro to Lafayette	31 C12	15	SR 18 bridge	Davis Ferry Park	Enjoyable trip in summer. River mostly bordered by green fields and forest. Some high bluffs. Last 6 miles on Wabash River after two rivers join.
Vernon Fork of Muscatatuck River, Vernon to Seymour	52 E2	21.5	Town park	US 31 bridge	Limestone bluffs border winding river for 3–4 miles. Rock bottom changes to soft silt further downstream. Possible takeout at CR 400W bridge at mile 8. Passes southern boundary of Muscatatuck National Wildlife Refuge.
Wabash River, Huntington to Terre Haute	28 G4	192	Below dam	Fairbanks Park access site	Slow-moving, muddy river drains state's fertile farmland. Wooded banks, several islands and Hanging Rock among sights in first 24 miles. Some riffles. Camping.
West Fork of White River, Martinsville to Bloomfield	44 F4	67.5	SR 39 bridge	River Road bridge west of town	Diverse scenery includes hill country, forest and wetlands. Moderate flow increases after Elno due to many tributaries. Camping at McCormicks Creek State Park.
Whitewater River, Cambridge City to Harrison, Ohio	41 H7	64	Crietz Park	Jameson Road bridge south of town	River one of swiftest in state with average gradient of 6 feet per mile. Popular section from quaint town of Metamora to state line crowded in summer.

Historic Sites

ANGEL MOUNDS STATE HISTORIC SITE – Evansville – 61 F10 103-acre active excavation site of prehistoric Mississippian settlement inhabited A.D. 900–1200. Reconstructed temple, stockade wall and homes built on mounds. Nature preserve. Interpretive center with exhibits.

BEN-HUR MUSEUM – Crawfordsville – 37 D11 1896 brick and limestone building that served as General Lew Wallace's private study. *Ben-Hur: A Tale of the Christ* author and Civil War hero became ambassador, senator and governor. Personal and wartime memorabilia.

BONNEYVILLE MILL – Bristol – 21 A12 Built mid-1820s, oldest continuously operating gristmill in state still stone-grinds flour daily, May through October. Surrounded by 222-acre county park. Historical programs.

COLONEL WILLIAM JONES STATE HISTORIC SITE – Gentryville – 62 C3 Carefully restored Federal-style home of Civil War Colonel William Jones. Abraham Lincoln thought to have performed odd jobs for Jones family in 1820s. Surrounded by 100-acre forest.

CONNER PRAIRIE – Fishers – 39 E9 Living-history museum comprised of restored 1823 Federal-style brick home of fur trader William Conner, 1836 Prairietown, 1886 Liberty Corner, 1816 Lenape Camp and hands-on PastPort area. Museum. Guided tours.

COPSHAHOLM – South Bend – 20 B6 Also known as the Oliver Mansion, magnificent 38-room stone home of Joseph Oliver built 1895–1896. Original furnishings. Over 2 acres of landscaped grounds with formal garden. Guided tours.

CORYDON CAPITOL STATE HISTORIC SITE – Corydon – 64 A2 Federal-style building was first state capitol. Built 1814–1816 (of local poplar, walnut and blue limestone) after first territorial capital moved from Vincennes in 1813. Nearby "Constitution Elm" still stands. Guided tours.

CULBERTSON MANSION STATE HISTORIC SITE – New Albany – 58 H6 25-room Second Empire–style mansion built 1867 by businessman William S. Culbertson. Opulent Victorian-era lifestyle reflected in hand-painted ceilings, carved rosewood staircase, marble fireplaces and crystal chandeliers.

ERNIE PYLE STATE HISTORIC SITE – Dana – 36 H4 Birthplace home of Pulitzer Prize–winning, WWII journalist Ernie Pyle. Birthplace home and authentic WWII-era Quonset huts, moved to present location, contain mementos of his life and writings. Visitor center.

EUGENE V DEBS HOME – Terre Haute – 42 E5 Midwestern Victorian–style home of Socialist Party and labor leader who ran for US presidency five times. Eight-room home built 1890. Period furnishings, campaign memorabilia. Murals by John Joseph Laska.

FORKS OF THE WABASH HISTORIC PARK – Huntington – 28 G3 Living-history museum on 96 acres. Main house built by Miami Chief John B. Richardville at time of treaty negotiations in 1830s. One-room schoolhouse. Museum has treaty papers, and pioneer and Indian dress.

GENE STRATTON–PORTER STATE HISTORIC SITE – Rome City – 22 E5 Log cabin, built 1914, was second home of author–naturalist Gene Statton–Porter. Original furnishings, memorabilia and photographs. Library. Wildflower gardens.

GEORGE ROGERS CLARK NATIONAL HISTORICAL PARK – Vincennes – 55 B9 Granite and marble memorial overlooking Wabash River marks site where General George Rogers Clark led ragtag troops in capture of Ft Sackville from British. Murals and audiovisual presentation. Visitor center.

GROUSELAND – Vincennes – 55 B9 Also known as Harrison Mansion. Home of 9th US President William Henry Harrison from 1803–1812, when he served as first governor of Indiana Territory. Georgian-style brick mansion contains some original furnishings.

HISTORIC FT WAYNE – Ft Wayne – 29 D8 Area named for Revolutionary War General "Mad Anthony" Wayne. Notable sites include replica of 1815 Historic Ft Wayne, Johnny Appleseed Memorial Park, 1902 Allen County Courthouse. Several historic districts.

HISTORIC MADISON – Madison – 59 A11 19th-century Ohio River port and railway center home to many notable historic landmarks. Shrewsbury–Windle House features free-standing spiral staircase. Formal gardens at elegant Lanier Mansion State Historic Site. Self-guided walking tours.

JAMES WHITCOMB RILEY BIRTHPLACE – Greenfield – 39 H12 Boyhood home and adjacent museum display memorabilia of well-known poet's life. Riley (1849–1916) authored many popular poems, most inspired by a colorful childhood and love of local surroundings. Guided tours.

JAMES WHITCOMB RILEY HOUSE – Indianapolis – 39 H8 Well-preserved Victorian home where Hoosier poet was boarder 1893–1916. Many personal possessions, even Riley's pen, on display. Located in Lockerbie Square neighborhood among other restored Victorian homes.

LANIER MANSION STATE HISTORIC SITE – Madison – 59 A11 1844 Greek Revival–style home of financier James F. D. Lanier, who loaned more than

$1 million to support Indiana's Civil War regiments. Three-story spiral staircase. Gardens. Guided tours.

LEVI COFFIN HOUSE STATE HISTORIC SITE – Fountain City – 41 E10 Federal-style brick home was major station on Underground Railroad 1839–1847. Quakers Levi and Catherine Coffin helped more than 2,000 escaped slaves reach safety. Period furnishings.

LIMBERLOST STATE HISTORIC SITE – Geneva – 35 C10 Log cabin home to author, naturalist and photographer Gene Stratton Porter, 1895–1913. Here she wrote six novels and studied flora and fauna of Limberlost Swamp. Original furnishings and memorabilia.

LINCOLN BOYHOOD NATIONAL MEMORIAL – Gentryville – 62 C4 200-acre site preserves farm where young Abraham Lincoln lived with family 1816–1830. Reconstructed, working pioneer farm. Burial site of Lincoln's mother. Audiovisual presentation. Visitor center.

MANSFIELD ROLLER MILL STATE HISTORIC SITE – Mansfield – 43 B8 Wooden mill built in 1880. Original equipment, including turbines used to power mill, remains intact.

MOUNDS STATE PARK – Anderson – 40 C2 Ten distinct earthworks constructed circa 150 B.C. by Adena and Hopewell people. Great Mound largest and best-preserved. Variously shaped mounds likely constructed for ceremonial and burial purposes. Trails.

NEW HARMONY STATE HISTORIC SITE – New Harmony – 60 C4 Site preserves two of America's earliest utopian communities: Harmonie on the Wabash (1814–1824) and New Harmony (1825–1826) founded by Scottish socialist Robert Owen. Features include Harmonist community house, Thrall's Opera House and labyrinth. Tours leave from The Atheneum.

PIGEON ROOST STATE HISTORIC SITE – Scottsburg – 58 C6 Limestone obelisk memorializes 24 settlers of Pigeon Roost killed on September 3, 1812 raid by Native Americans who supported British in War of 1812. First of several conflicts in Indiana Territory.

PRESIDENT BENJAMIN HARRISON HOME – Indianapolis – 39 H8 Restored 16-room brick Italianate mansion home to 23rd US President and family 1875–1901. Museum in third-floor ballroom displays artifacts of Harrisons' professional and personal lives. Period furnishings. Guided tours.

SPRING MILL STATE PARK – Mitchell – 57 A11 Reconstructed 1800s pioneer village centered around still-functional water-powered gristmill. Log houses, tavern, cemetery, cave system. Virgil I. Grissom Memorial honors native and one of seven original US astronauts. Camping, hiking, swimming.

STATE CAPITOL – Indianapolis – 39 H8 Restored 1880s Renaissance Revival structure built of Indiana limestone. Houses executive, legislative and judicial offices. Guided tours.

T C STEELE STATE HISTORIC SITE – Belmont – 50 C5 211-acre site features home and studio of Indiana artist Theodore Clement Steele. Changing exhibits of Steele's impressionist paintings. Hiking trails, wildflower gardens and 92-acre nature preserve. Guided tours.

TIPPECANOE BATTLEFIELD NATIONAL HISTORIC LANDMARK – Lafayette – 31 E11 Site where, on November 7, 1811, troops under General William Henry Harrison defeated coalition led by legendary Shawnee chief Tecumseh and his brother, The Prophet. Museum exhibits. Hiking trails. Nature center.

VINCENNES STATE HISTORIC SITES – Vincennes – 55 B9 State's oldest city and first capitol of Indiana Territory. Historic sites include 1805 capitol building, replica of first print shop, birthplace home of author Maurice Stout, 1838 bank building and fort that served as 1803–1813 military outpost.

WHITEWATER CANAL STATE HISTORIC SITE – Metamora – 47 F8 Restored 14-mile section of original 76-mile-long waterway built 1836–1847. Features working gristmill, horse-drawn canal boat *Ben Franklin III* and nation's only working covered aqueduct. Boat rides.

WILBUR WRIGHT BIRTHPLACE – Millville – 41 E7 Restored birthplace home of aviation pioneer exhibits family memorabilia and life-size replica of Wright Flyer. Wilbur (1867–1912) and his brother Orville Wright (1871–1948) built and flew first successful aircraft in 1903.

Wildlife Viewing

Indiana takes part in the National Watchable Wildlife Program, a program in which state, federal and private organizations have joined forces and combined funds to promote wildlife viewing, conservation and education. This chart includes wildlife areas in Indiana as listed and detailed in the Indiana Wildlife Viewing Guide, *published by Falcon Press.*

The chart's indicator columns are grouped under **WILDLIFE** (with a **BIRDS** sub-group) and include: Amphibians/Reptiles; Birds of Prey; Perching Songbirds; Shorebirds; Wading; Waterfowl; Freshwater Fish; Hoofed Mammals; Carnivores; Small Mammals; Wildflowers; Barrier-Free Access; Boating; Hiking; Cross-Country Skiing.

NAME, LOCATION	PAGE & GRID	ACREAGE/MILEAGE
Avoca State Fish Hatchery, Avoca	50 F3	43
Bixler Lake Park Wetland Nature Area, Kendallville	23 F7	82
Bluespring Caverns, Bedford	50 H3	15
Bonneyville Mill County Park, Bristol	21 A12	223
Brown County State Park, Nashville	51 B7	15,696
Buzzards Roost Overlook, Magnet	63 C10	80
Cass County France Park, Logansport	32 A4	400
Chain O'Lakes State Park, Burr Oak	22 G5	2,678
Clifty Falls State Park, Madison	59 A11	1,360
Crosley Fish and Wildlife Area, Vernon	52 E2	4,000
Deep River County Park, Ainsworth	19 E7	1,000
Delaney Creek Park/Knobstone Trail, Salem	58 A3	354/58 mi
Dobbs Park, Terre Haute	42 E5	105
Eagle Creek Park, Indianapolis	38 G6	5,250
Falls of the Ohio National Wildlife Conservation Area, Jeffersonville	58 H6	68
Fox Island County Park, Ft Wayne	29 D7	605
Gibson Lake Wildlife Habitat, Princeton	54 F6	160
Gibson Woods Nature Preserve, Hammond	18 C4	130
Glendale Fish and Wildlife Area, Montgomery	56 D3	8,000
Griffy Reservoir, Bloomington	50 B3	1,200
Hall Woods Nature Preserve, Bainbridge	43 A12	94
Harmonie State Park, New Harmony	60 C4	3,465
Hayes Regional Arboretum, Richmond	41 G11	355
Hickory Ridge Trails, Bloomington	50 D5	60 mi
Hoosier Prairie Nature Preserve, Griffith	18 D4	439
Hovey Lake, Mt Vernon	60 H4	4,400
Imagination Glen Park, Portage	19 C8	223
Indian/Celina Lakes, St Croix	63 B8	12
Indiana Dunes National Lakeshore, Porter	19 C9	13,945
Indiana Dunes State Park, Dune Acres	19 B9	2,182
Jasper–Pulaski Fish and Wildlife Area, Medaryville	25 C10	8,022
Kankakee River Fish and Wildlife Area, Knox	20 H1	3,328
Kekionga Park, Decatur	29 H11	55
Kekionga Trail, Markle	28 G4	10 mi
Killbuck Wetland, Anderson	40 C1	3
Kingsbury Fish and Wildlife Area, La Porte	20 D2	5,000
Kokomo Reservoir, Kokomo	33 E9	800
LaSalle Fish and Wildlife Area, Lake Village	24 B4	3,648
Little Blue River, Sulphur	63 A10	14 mi
Luhr County Park, La Porte	20 C1	73
Maines Pond, Freetown	51 D7	5
Majenica Marsh, Huntington	28 H3	7
Maplewood Nature Center, LaGrange	22 C6	68
Mary Gray Bird Sanctuary, Connersville	47 C7	660
McCormicks Creek State Park, Spencer	44 H1	1,833
Merry Lea Environmental Center, Wolf Lake	22 H3	1,150
Migrant Trap, Hammond	18 B3	16
Minnehaha Fish and Wildlife Area, Sullivan	48 C5	11,500
Mishawaka Fish Ladder, Mishawaka	21 B7	0.5
Mississinewa Lake, Peru	33 B12	14,000
Mt Baldy, Michigan City	19 B9	90
Muscatatuck County Park, Vernon	52 E2	260
Muscatatuck National Wildlife Refuge Auto Tour, Seymour	51 E12	3 mi
Nappanee Environmental Education Area, Nappanee	21 E10	35
North Fork Marsh Complex, Bloomington	50 C5	500
Oak Leaf Trail, Vallonia	51 H9	4.1 mi
Oak Ridge Prairie County Park, Griffith	18 D5	695
Old Camp Atterbury, Edinburgh	45 G9	6,000
Ouabache Trails Park, Vincennes	55 A9	254
Patoka Lake Overlook, French Lick	57 F8	1
Paw Paw Marsh, Shoals	57 C7	5
Pigeon River Fish and Wildlife Area, Mongo	22 B6	11,500
Portland Arch Nature Preserve, Fountain	36 A5	292
Potato Creek State Park, North Liberty	20 D5	3,840
Potawatomi Wildlife Park, Bourbon	27 A8	203
Raccoon State Recreation Area, Rockville	43 A9	4,065
Riddle Point Park, Bloomington	50 A5	100
River Preserve County Park, Benton	21 D12	1,000
Round Lake Wetland Conservation Area and Nature Preserve, Bass Lake	26 A2	140
Rum Village Woods, South Bend	20 B6	160
Scales Lake Park, Boonville	61 D12	400
Shades State Park, Alamo	37 F9	3,082
Shakamak State Park, Jasonville	49 B7	1,766
Spicer Lake Nature Preserve, New Carlisle	20 A3	240
Spring Mill State Park, Mitchell	57 A11	1,319
Summit Lake State Park, Rogersville	40 D6	2,552
Switchgrass Marshes, Huntington	34 A2	11
Sycamore Creek Marsh, French Lick	57 G9	20
Three Lakes Trail, Martinsville	44 H4	10 mi
Tippecanoe River State Park, Beardstown	26 C2	2,761
Tri-County Fish and Wildlife Area, North Webster	22 G1	3,400
Turkey Run State Park, Marshall	37 G7	2,382
Twin Swamps Nature Preserve, Hovey	60 H4	585
Versailles State Park, Versailles	53 D7	5,905
Wabash Heritage Trail, Lafayette	31 E11	7.5 mi
Wesselman Woods Nature Preserve, Evansville	61 E9	200
White River Parks, Indianapolis	39 G8	83
Wyandotte Woods, Leavenworth	63 B12	2,100
Yellowwood State Forest, Belmont	50 B5	22,500

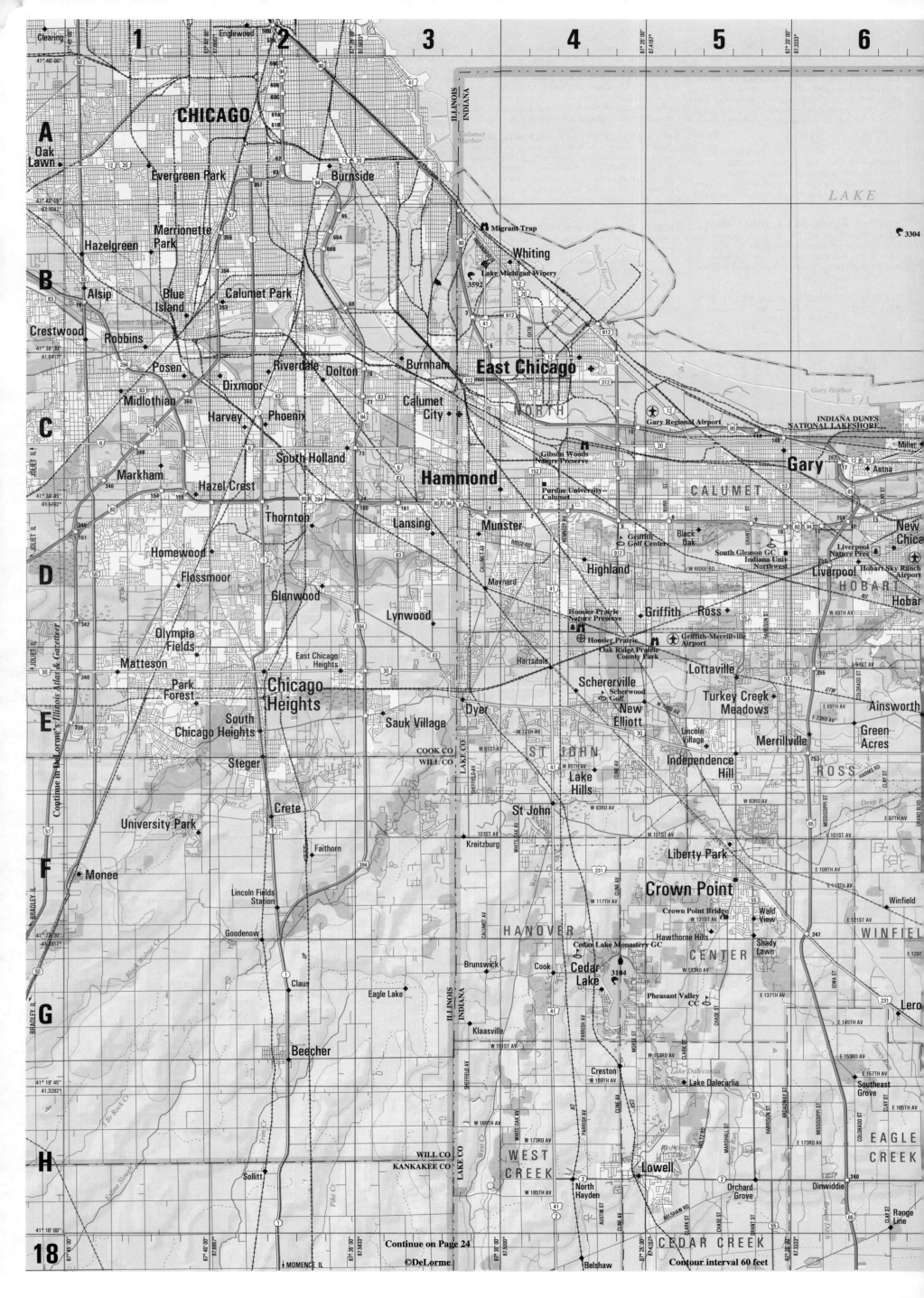

Continue on Page 24

©DeLorme

Contour interval 60 feet

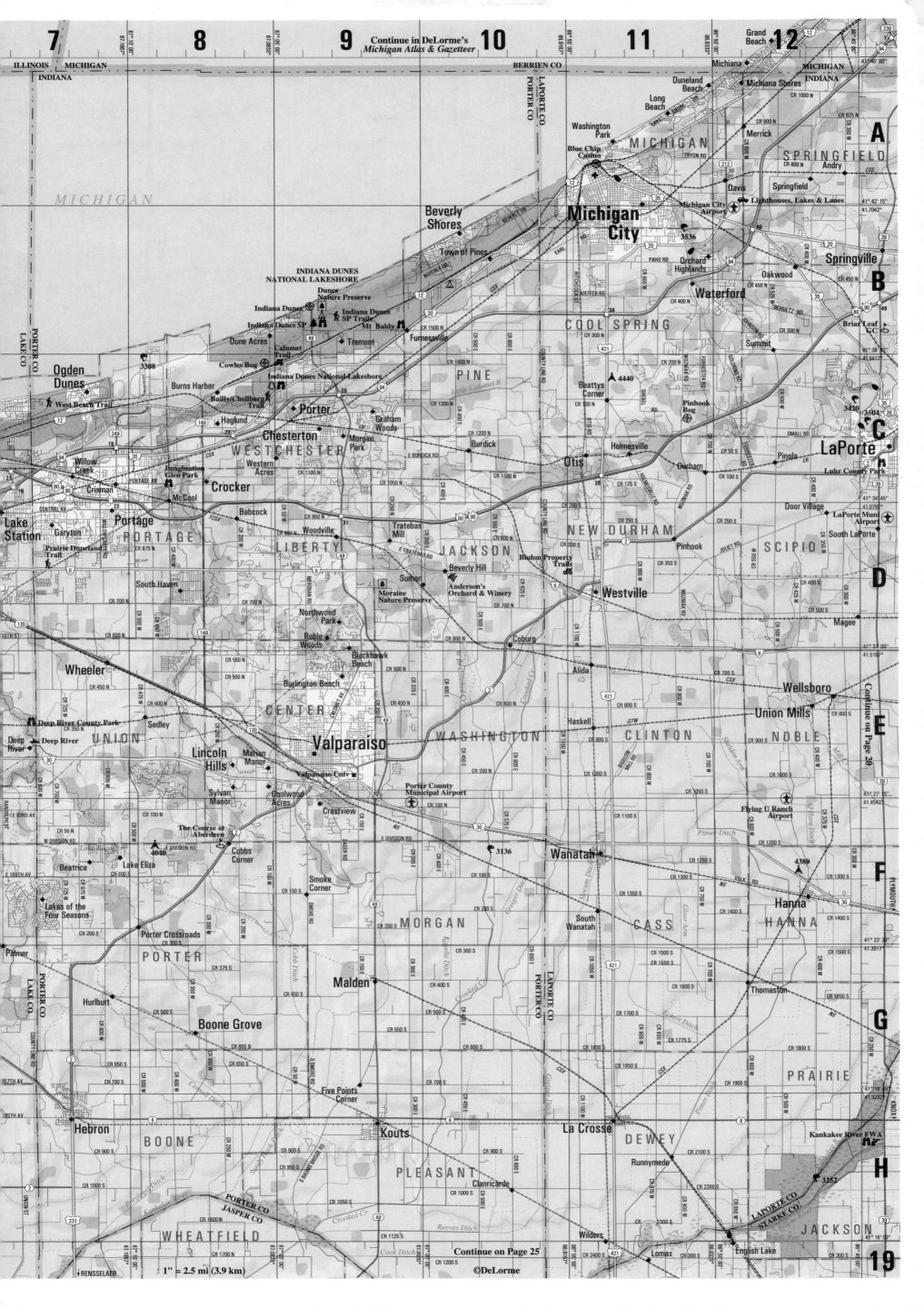

Continue in DeLorme's
Michigan Atlas & Gazetteer

Berrien Springs MI

BERRIEN CO

Spicer Lake Nature Preserve

MICHIGAN
INDIANA

SPRINGFIELD

Hesston

HUDSON

LaPORTE CO
ST JOSEPH CO

Bertrand
State Line

Dutch
Corners

GALENA

CR 1000 N

Hamilton

German

Portage

Blackthorn GC

Roselan
St Mary's

Andry
Lalimere   Smith
Hillside   Birchim   Hicks
Lake Park

Hudson
Lake

Plainfield

Chain-O-Lakes

Olive   Zeigler
Lydick
Ardmore

Michiana Regional
Transportation Center Airport

Northern Indiana
Center for History

Galena WCA
Springfield Fen
Nature Preserve

New Carlisle

OLIVE

Springville

Rolling Prairie

Byron

WILLS

Finger
Lake

Hum Lake

Clear Lake

Westfield

WARREN

Chamberlain

Copshah
Studeb
National

CENTER

Briar Leaf GC

3420   3120
3504

KANKAKEE

Crumstown

GREENE

CENTER

Nutwood

LaPorte

Monroe Manor

PLEASANT

LINCOLN

Mill Creek

Kline Tr
Roosevelt Rd
Layton Rd

Rum Village
Woods

Gilmer Pa

Luhr County
Park

Beechwood GC

Door Prairie
Auto Museum

Salem Heights

3188

Fish Lake

Fish Lake
WCA

Kankakee R

Kale
Lake

Potato Creek SP
Trails   3596

Swamp Rose
Nature Preserve

Colburn

Door
Village

LaPorte Municipal Airport

South
LaPorte

SCIPIO

Stillwell

Lower
Fish Lake

3428

Potato Creek SP

4020

Magee

Kingsbury

Kingsbury FWA

North
Liberty

Pine

Lakeville

3424

KINGSBURY
FISH AND WILDLIFE AREA

Kankakee

LIBERTY

UNION

Continue on Page 19

WASHINGTON

Kankakee River

LINCOLN

Tracy

Union Center

ST JOSEPH CO
MARSHALL CO

Kingsford
Heights

South
Center

Teegarden

La Paz

La Paz Jct

NOBLE

Walkerton

UNION

JOHNSON

STARKE CO

Koontz Lake Nature Preserve

POLK

NORTH

HANNA

Robbins Rd

3264

Koontz Lake

Tyner

Harris
Linkville

DAVIS

Hamlet

Hamlet GC

OREGON

4120   Grovertown

Plymouth Rock GC

PRAIRIE

Donaldson

4710

Plymouth Municipal Airport

Brems

Starke County Airport

WEST

Plymouth

CENTER

WASHINGTON

Menominee WCA

CENTER

LaPORTE CO
STARKE CO

Kankakee River
FWA

3600

Knox

Twin Lakes

3364

JACKSON

Ober

UNION

Continue on Page 26

©DeLorme

Toto

LOGANSPORT

Burr Oak

GREEN

Contour interval 60 feet

7   **8**   **9**   **10**   **11**   **12**

Continue in DeLorme's *Michigan Atlas & Gazetteer*

NILES MI   MOTTVILLE MI   MOTTVILLE MI

BERRIEN CO   CASS CO

MICHIGAN / INDIANA   CASS CO   MICHIGAN / INDIANA   CASS CO   ST JOSEPH CO

ST JOSEPH CO   ELKHART CO

41° 46′ 00″

Allenton

Simonton Lake

Granger   4590

3468

4140

Pipewort Pond Nature Preserve

A

CLAY   HARRIS   CLEVELAND   OSOLO   WASHINGTON   YORK

Elkhart   Heritage Trail

Juday Creek GC   Elkhart Municipal Airport   St Joseph River   Bristol   Bonneyville Mill   Bonneyville Mill County Park

Nibbyville

Douglas Rd   Pleasant Valley

Univ of Notre Dame   Maple Lane

South Bend   Ruthmere Mus

3128   Midwest Museum of American Art   Old Orchard GC

Bethel Coll   **Elkhart**   41° 42′ 15″ / 41.7042°

B

East Race Waterway   College Football Hall of Fame

Indiana Univ–South Bend   Eberhart Municipal GC   3496   Osceola   Glenwood   Mishawaka Pilots Club Airport   Lusher Av

Mishawaka Fish Ladder   **Mishawaka**   Hively St   JEFFERSON   MIDDLEBURY

PENN   BAUGO   Mishawaka Rd

41° 38′ 30″ / 41.6417°

Dunlap   CONCORD   Midway

Jamestown   **C**

Rogers Ditch   Grimes Ditch

Goshen

Woodland   OLIVE   HARRISON   Black Squirrel GC   Taste of Honeyville Trail   CLINTON

41° 34′ 45″ / 41.5792°

D

MADISON   Wakarusa   Southwest   ELKHART   Goshen Coll   Waterford Mills

UNION   Wyatt   **Wakarusa**   Yellow Creek Lake   Goshen Municipal Airport   Goshen Dam Pond

Midway Corners   Foraker   River Preserve County Park   3180   41° 31′ 00″ / 41.5167°

LOCKE   UNION   New Paris   3476   **E**

ST JOSEPH CO / MARSHALL CO   Locke   JACKSON   BENTON

Nappanee Environmental Education Area

Amish Acres / Round Barn Theater   McCormicks Creek GC   Nappanee Municipal Airport   ELKHART CO / KOSCIUSKO CO

Bremen   Nappanee   Gravelton   Syracuse   3524   **F**

4530   3312   **Nappanee**   Berlin Court Ditch   Milford Junction   Wawasee Golf & CC

GERMAN   SCOTT   JEFFERSON   Milford   Oakwood Park

Lake of the Woods   Shady Banks   41° 25′ 30″ / 41.3917°

Hastings   Wabee Lake   Redmon Park   TURKEY CREEK

Dausman Ditch   3148   Quaker Haven Park   **G**

VAN BUREN   Dewart Lake   TIPPECANOE

CENTER   BOURBON   Leesburg   4500   Bell Rohr Park   Walker Park   Mineral Springs

Inwood   Clunette   Oswego   3212

PLAIN

Bourbon   ETNA   PRAIRIE   Monoquet   Island Park   3036   Arrowhead Park   **H**

Etna Green   4230   Big Chapman Lake Nature Preserve   Warsaw Muni Airport   Little Chapman Lake Nature Preserve   3336

WALNUT   Hoffman Lake   WAYNE   41° 16′ 00″

TIPPECANOE   1″ = 2.5 mi (3.9 km)

Continue on Page 27   Atwood   ©DeLorme

Continue on Page 22

21

ST JOSEPH CO
MICHIGAN
INDIANA

ST JOSEPH CO ' BRANCH CO
LAGRANGE CO

A
MI
IN Vistula
York
Oak Hills GC
4130
4150
Bonneyville Mills
4560
Fawn River
Star Mill
Cedar Lake GC
3096
VAN BUREN
Scott
Twin Lakes
4580
4520
3484
4660
LIMA
Howe
GREENFIELD
Brighton
Ontario
3416
Mongo
Pigeon River FWA
Pigeon River

B
Middlebury
Middlebury
3340
3088
3460
Shipshewana
Menno-Hof
4570
CLAY
BLOOMFIELD
SPRINGFIELD
Tamarack Bog
Tamarack Bog Nature Preserve
Plato
3540

C
MIDDLEBURY
NEWBURY
Lagrange
Emma
3448
Honeyville
Maplewood Nature Center
3192
CLINTON
EDEN
CLEARSPRING
Valentine
Woodruff
3392
3388
JOHNSON
MILFORD
Olin Lake Nature Preserve
3000

D
Stony Creek
Topeka
Eddy
3008
3588
South Milford
Millersburg
LAGRANGE CO / NOBLE CO
Wolcottville

E
Benton
3180
Elkhart River
Grismore
BENTON
PERRY
ELKHART
Cosperville
Rome City
3568
ORANGE
3132
WAYNE
Gene Stratton–Porter SHS
Kendallville Municipal Airport
Ligonier
Wawaka
Brimfield
3124
Wakeville Village
Hoffman

F
Mallard Roost WCA
3152
Eagle Lake WCA
3168
Syracuse
3524
Wawasee Golf & CC
Wawasee
Oakwood Park
Wawasee Wetlands Nature Preserve
3328
Kendallville
JEFFERSON
ALBION
3472
Lisbon
ALLEN

G
Sunrise Beach
South Park
TURKEY CREEK
Marineland Gardens
Enchanted Hills
Indian Village
Quaker Haven Park
Tri-County FWA
Cromwell
Kimmell
SPARTA
YORK
Augusta Hills GC
South Branch of Elkhart River
Albion
Port Mitchell
Bakerstown
Chain O'Lakes SP
Egans Point
Chain O'Lakes SP Trails

H
Epworth Forest
3564
Mineral Springs
North Webster
3212
3256
Washington Center
Highbanks
Yellowbanks
Wilmot
WASHINGTON
3020
Wolf Lake
Burr Oak
GREEN
Green Center
SWAN
3456
Barbee
3268
Lakeview Spring
Bayfield
TIPPECANOE
KOSCIUSKO CO / NOBLE CO WHITLEY CO
Merry Lea Environmental Center
Ormas
ETNA TROY
Etna
3352
3040
NOBLE
Merriam
3140
Crooked Lake Nature Preserve
NOBLE CO / WHITLEY CO
4690
NORTH MANCHESTER

Continue on Page 21
Continue on Page 28

©DeLorme

Contour interval 60 feet

FT WAYNE

MICHIGAN / INDIANA
Ray   BRANCH CO
Camden

A

Greenfield Mills   MILLGROVE   Jamestown   Clear Lake   Cedar Swamp WCA   Fremont   FREMONT
Orland   3184   3560   Nevada Mills   Panama   CLEAR LAKE
Pigeon River FWA   JACKSON   Glen Eden   Lake James GC   PLEASANT   SCOTT   YORK   Page   York   Billingstown

B

Brushy Prairie   Flint   Loon Lake Nature Preserve   3144   3412   Cooney
Columbia

Tri-State–Steuben Co Airport   Zollner GC   Angola   Tri-State Univ   Ellis   Berlein   Courtney Corner

C

Mt Pisgah   Wildwood   Elmira   Stroh   Salem Center   Moonlight   OTSEGO   Metz
3344   3052   3208

Shady Nook   Gravel Beach   Timberhurst   SALEM   STEUBEN   Pleasant Lake   Alvarado   RICHLAND   Edon
Turkey Creek   Otsego Center   Cold Springs

D

Helmer   Hudson   Steubenville   Forest Park   Oakwood   Hamilton
LAGRANGE CO / STEUBEN CO   NOBLE CO / DEKALB CO   Ashley   3012   STEUBEN CO / DEKALB CO

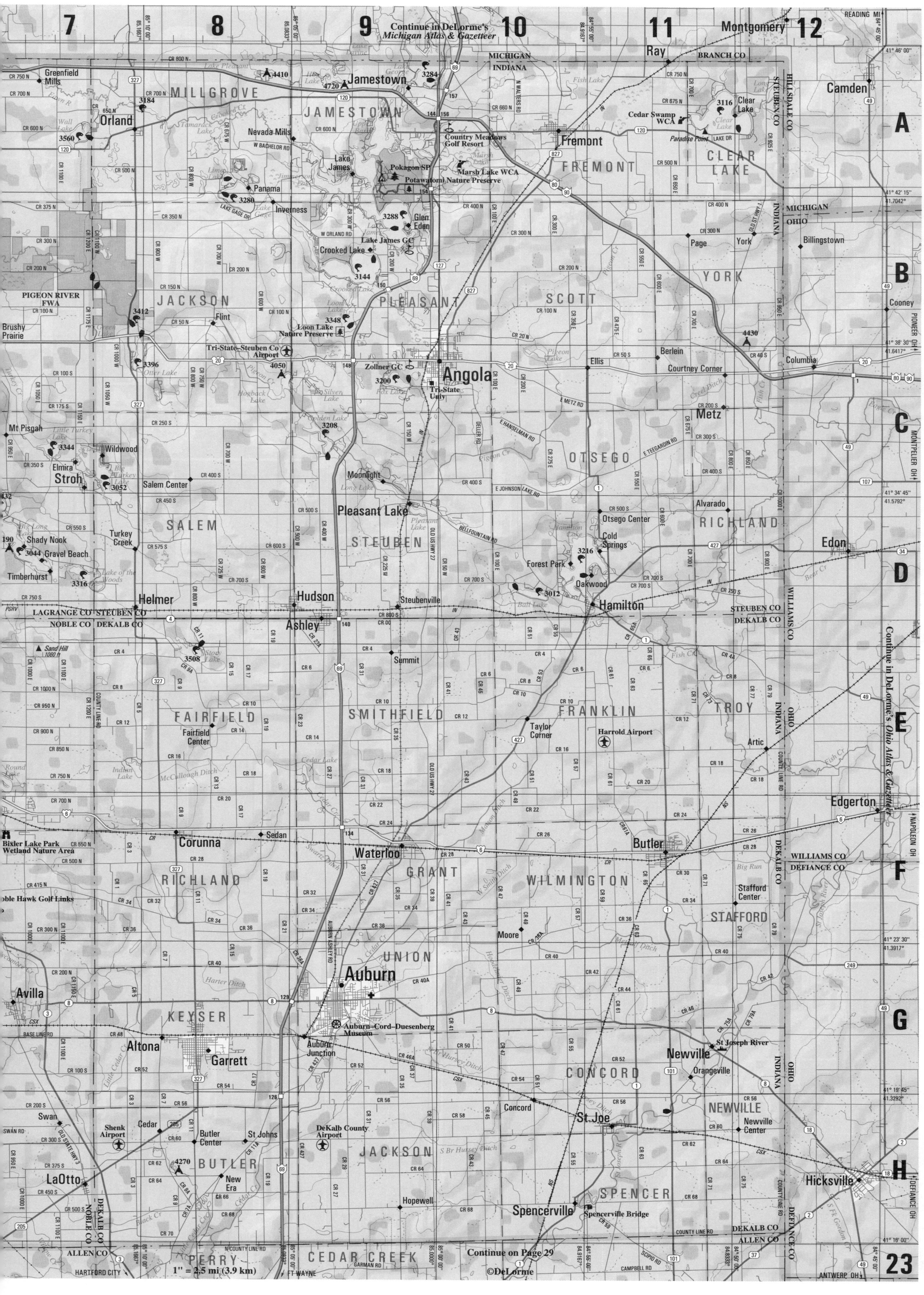

Sand Hill   Summit   FAIRFIELD   SMITHFIELD   FRANKLIN   TROY
Fairfield Center   Taylor Corner   Harrold Airport   Artic

E

Edgerton   OHIO / INDIANA

Bixler Lake Park Wetland Nature Area   Corunna   Sedan   Waterloo   GRANT   WILMINGTON   Butler   WILLIAMS CO / DEFIANCE CO
RICHLAND   Stafford Center   STAFFORD

F

Noble Hawk Golf Links   Moore

Avilla   UNION   Auburn   KEYSER   Auburn-Cord-Duesenberg Museum
Altona   Garrett   Auburn Junction   Newville   Orangeville   CONCORD   St Joseph River

G

Swan   Cedar   Butler Center   St Johns   DeKalb County Airport   Concord   St. Joe   Newville Center
Shenk Airport   JACKSON

LaOtto   BUTLER   New Era   SPENCER   Hicksville
Hopewell   Spencerville   Spencerville Bridge

H

DEKALB CO / ALLEN CO   PERRY   CEDAR CREEK   Continue on Page 29   ©DeLorme   ANTWERP OH
Hartford City   FT WAYNE   1" = 2.5 mi (3.9 km)

23

Continue on Page 18

Continue on Page 30

PORTER CO
LAKE CO

MICHIGAN CITY
LAPORTE

WHEATFIELD

PLEASANT

Continue on Page 19

Wilders
Lomax
English Lake

RAILROAD

WAYNE

North Judson

Demotte
Kersey Stoutsburg
Wheatfield

KANKAKEE

Dunns
Dunns Bridge

San Pierre
Tefft

STARKE CO
PULASKI CO

KEENER

Stoutsburg Savanna
Nature Preserve

Deer Park
Zadoc
Kniman

WALKER

JASPER-PULASKI
FISH & WILDLIFE AREA

Radioville

CASS
RICH GROVE

Virgie

Wolf Cr

Jasper-Pulaski FWA

Clarks

Moffitt

Laura

Asphaltum

Medaryville

UNION

Gifford

Baileys
Corner

GILLAM

WHITE POST
JEFFERSON

Parr Rosebud
Aix

Newland

BARKLEY Lewiston

Surrey

DIVISION RD

Moody RD
Moody

Francesville

SALEM

NEWTON
Jasper County
Airport

North Marion

HANGING GROVE

BEAVER

Rensselaer

Pleasant
Ridge

Hanging
Grove

Lakeside

St Josephs Coll
MARION
South Marion

JASPER CO PULASKI CO
WHITE CO

Collegeville

McCoysburg

Lee

Buffalo

JORDAN

MILROY

Monon

MONON

Egypt

PRINCETON

LIBERTY

Sitka

CARPENTER

WHITE CO
JASPER CO

Fountain Park

HONEY CREEK

Tippecanoe CC
Guernsey

Indiana Beach

Remington

Wolcott

Continue on Page 31
©DeLorme

Norway
UNION

Monticello

1" = 2.5 mi (3.9 km)

25

LAPORTE   SOUTH BEND   PLYMOUTH   SOUTH BEND

Continue on Page 20

A

Toto

Round Lake WCA &
Nature Preserve

WAYNE   CALIFORNIA   NORTH BEND

Winona

3016

Cranberry Point

Bass Lake State Beach

Cedar Point

Bass Lake

Ober

Yellow River

Burr Lake

Hibbard

Rutland

UNION   GREEN

Culver

Maxinkuckee

Lake Maxinkuckee

3300

Lena Park

Aldine

Hook Ditch

Wheeler Airport

Bass

Ora

B

STARKE CO
PULASKI CO

Denham

Sandhill Nature Preserve

Monterey

PULASKI CO / STARKE CO

FULTON CO / MARSHALL CO

Delong

Richland Center

RICHLAND

RICH GROVE

FRANKLIN

Beardstown

TIPPECANOE

AUBBEENAUBBEE

Leiters Ford

C

Winamac FWA

Tippecanoe River SP

Tippecanoe River Nature Preserve

Sand Ridge Trail

Ripley

Arens Field

Lawton

Vanmeter Park

Pershing

3076
4250

Guise Park

Lake Bruce

Bruce Lake

ROCHESTER

Little Mill Cr

D

Winamac

JEFFERSON

MONROE

HARRISON

UNION

Kewanna

Moss Creek CC

Continue on Page 25

E

Berns–Meyer Nature Preserve

Pulaski

Star City

VAN BUREN

WAYNE

LIBERTY

Fulton

STAR CITY RD

BEAVER   INDIAN CREEK

Lakeside

Grass Creek

Marshtown

F

Thornhope

PULASKI CO
WHITE CO

FULTON CO
CASS CO

Fletcher

Fletcher Lake

G

Buffalo

Headlee

CASS

BOONE

HARRISON

BETHLEHEM

Metea

Bell Center

Royal Center

Lucerne

Leases Corner

LIBERTY

Mt Pleasant

H

Sitka

Verona

NOBLE

CLAY

Adamsboro

Old Adamsboro

LINCOLN

JACKSON

JEFFERSON

Norway

UNION

Lake Shafer

Idaville

Burnettsville

Lake Cicott

Trimer

Kenneth

Cass County
France Park

France Park Trails

Dunkirk

Logansport

Ironhorse GC

Continue on Page 32

©DeLorme

Contour interval 60 feet

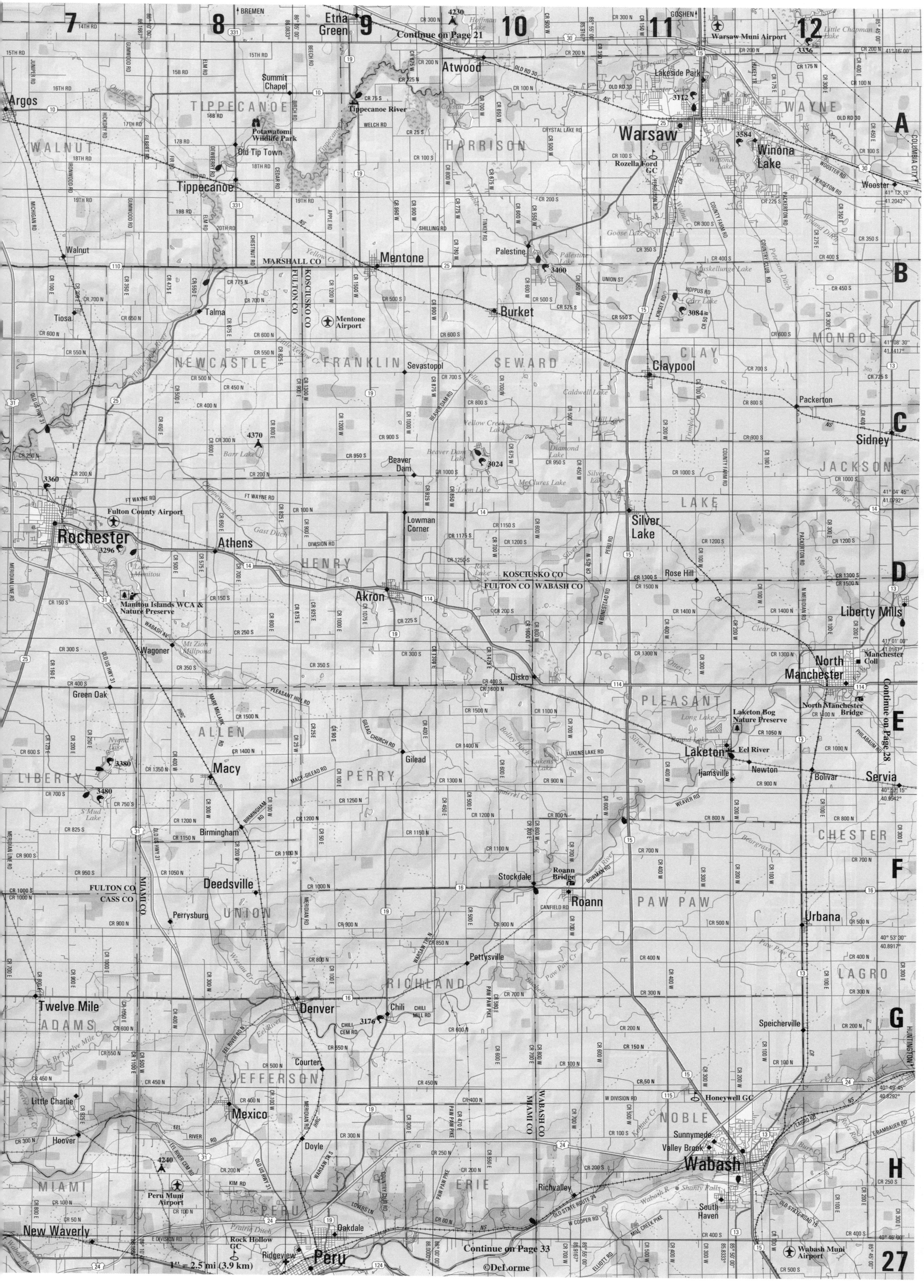

Continue on Page 21

BREMEN
Etna Green
4230
Hoffman Lake
Warsaw Muni Airport
Little Chapman Lake
GOSHEN
3336

Atwood
Summit Chapel
Tippecanoe River
Potawatomi Wildlife Park
Old Tip Town
TIPPECANOE
HARRISON
Lakeside Park
3112
Warsaw
3584
Winona Lake
Wooster
WAYNE

A

WALNUT
Tippecanoe
Rozella Ford GC
Goose Lake

Walnut
Mentone
MARSHALL CO
Palestine
3400
Palestine Lake
Muskellunge Lake
Hoppus Rd
Carr Lake

B

Tiosa
Talma
FULTON CO
KOSCIUSKO CO
Mentone Airport
Burket
3084
MONROE

NEWCASTLE
FRANKLIN
Sevastopol
SEWARD
Claypool
CLAY
Caldwell Lake

C

4370
Barr Lake
Beaver Dam
3024
Beaver Dam Lake
Yellow Creek Lake
Diamond Lake
Hill Lake
Silver Lake
Packerton
Sidney
JACKSON

3360
Fulton County Airport
Rochester
3296
Lake Manitou
Athens
HENRY
Lowman Corner
Rock Lake
Silver Lake
Silver Lake
Rose Hill
LAKE
Liberty Mills
D
KOSCIUSKO CO
FULTON CO   WABASH CO

Manitou Islands WCA & Nature Preserve
Wagoner
Mt Zion Millpond
Akron
Disko
North Manchester
Manchester Coll
North Manchester Bridge
E
PLEASANT
Long Lake
Laketon Bog Nature Preserve
Laketon
Eel River
Continue on Page 28

Green Oak
Nyona Lake
ALLEN
Macy
3380
Gilead
Bidley Bush
Lukens Lake
Round Lake
Ijamsville
Newton
Bolivar
Servia
F
LIBERTY
3480
S Mud Lake
PERRY

Birmingham
Roann Bridge
Stockdale
Roann
PAW PAW
CHESTER
Urbana

Deedsville
FULTON CO
CASS CO
Perrysburg
UNION
Pottysville
RICHLAND
G
Twelve Mile
ADAMS
Denver
3176
Chili
Chili Mill Rd
Speicherville
LAGRO
MIAMI CO

Little Charlie
Hoover
Mexico
Doyle
NOBLE
Sunnymede
Valley Brook
Wabash
Honeywell GC
H
4240
Peru Muni Airport
MIAMI
PERU
ERIE
Richvalley
South Haven
Shanty Falls

New Waverly
Rock Hollow GC
Ridgeview
Peru
Continue on Page 33
Oakdale
Wabash Muni Airport

1" = 2.5 mi (3.9 km)
©DeLorme

27

Continue on Page 22

Continue on Page 27

Continue on Page 34

1 Bayfield
2 Etna
3 3040 3352
4 LAGRANGE NOBLE CO
5 GREEN
6 SWAN NOBLE CO

Crooked Lake Nature Preserve
3140 Cedar Lake
3100 Tri Lakes
3464 Shrine Lake
3444 Round Lake
3064 Blue Lake
Churubusco

4690 Ridinger Lake
KOSCIUSKO CO
Deniston Resource Area
Robinson Lake
WASHINGTON
ETNA-TROY
Cresco
Cedar Lake Br
Troy Cedar Lake
Goose Lake
THORNCREEK
SMITH
EEL RIVER

A WABASH
CR 100 S
Wooster
Pierceton
Lorane
Five Points
Collins

B Larwill
RICHLAND
MONROE
Columbia City
COLUMBIA
Levert
Lake Everett

C Sidney
Kinsey
Walnut Corners
Coesse Corners
Coesse
UNION
Arcola
Arcola

D JACKSON
South Whitley
Collamer
CLEVELAND
Peabody Briggs Raber
WASHINGTON
Laud
JEFFERSON
Dunfee
KOSCIUSKO CO
WABASH CO
WHITLEY CO
Liberty Mills
Tunker
Washington Center
Saturn
Liberty Hills
Rolling Hills
Forest Ridge
Ellisville
Timbercrest

E WABASH
North Manchester
Manchester Coll
Sycamore GC
Luther
WHITLEY CO
HUNTINGTON CO
Goblesville
Bracken
CHESTER
Abolte

F Servia
Makin
WARREN
CLEAR CREEK
JACKSON
Roanoke
Roanoke Station
LAFAYETTE
Bippus
Mahon
ALLEN CO
WELLS CO
Zanesville

G DALLAS
Forks of the Wabash Historic Park
Huntington Coll
Huntington
Bowerstown
UNION
Andrews
HUNTINGTON
Kekionga Trail
Huntington Municipal Airport
Simpson
Wabash River SRA
Huntington SRA
J Edward Roush Lake Project
3232
J EDWARD ROUSH LAKE PROJECT
Markle

H Lagro
WABASH
Salamonie Lake Project
Harlansburg
Toledo
POLK
LANCASTER
ROCK CREEK
ROCK CREEK
SALAMONIE LAKE PROJECT
Majenica Marsh
Majenica
Rock Creek
Switchgrass Marshes
Salamonie Lake Project
3452
Lincolnville
MARION
©DeLorme
Continue on Page 34
Contour interval 60 feet
HARTFORD CITY
Rockford

28

NOBLE CO / DEKALB CO
ALLEN CO
DEKALB CO / ALLEN CO
DEFIANCE CO / PAULDING CO

HICKSVILLE OH

A

Hursh
Georgetown
Halls Corners
SPRINGFIELD
SCIPIO

Huntertown
PERRY
Cedar Canyons
CEDAR CREEK
Leo
3236
Springfield Center Rd

Cedar Shores
Hurshtown Reservoir

Royville
Cedarville
Grabill
Harlan
Cuba

B
Carrolls
3108
Antwerp
Pond-A-River GC

Dunn Mill
Academie
Wallen
MILAN
Milan Center
Bluecast
MAUMEE
Antwerp

Colonial Oaks GC
WASHINGTON
Sunnybrook Acres
Concordia Gardens
ST JOSEPH
Brookside Estates

Smith Field
Crestwood
Royal Oaks
Golden Acres
C
Ludwig Park
Sunnymeadow
Hacienda Village
Woodburn
Northcrest
Greendale
Maplewood Park
Thurman
Five Points

Rivergreenway Recreational Trail
Indiana Univ Purdue Univ
3492

Ft Wayne Children's Zoo
Science Central
North Highland
St Francis Coll
Ft Wayne
Lincoln Museum

Gar Creek

Westlawn
Foellinger-Freimann Botanical Conservatory
Historic Ft Wayne
Indiana Inst of Technology
Lakeside GC
Maumee Valley GC
River Haven
Edgerton
D

Westmoor
Sunnymede Woods
New Haven
JEFFERSON
JACKSON

Time Corners
Meadowbrook
Zulu

Country Club Gardens
Taylor University Ft Wayne Campus
Fairfax
Tillman
Townley
Baldwin
McGill

Indian Village
WAYNE
ADAMS
Maples
E
Lincolnshire
Westchester
Four Presidents Corners

Waynedale
Eastland Gardens
MONROE
Monroeville

Fox Island County Park
Avalon

Baerfield
PLEASANT
MARION
Boston Corner
Dixon

Nine Mile
Hessen Cassel
MADISON
East Liberty

Ft Wayne International Airport
Middletown
Hoagland
F
Yoder
Poe
Williams
UNION

ALLEN CO / WELLS CO   ADAMS CO

Wolfcale

Ossian
JEFFERSON
PREBLE
ROOT

Monmouth
G
Greenwood
Middlebury

Uniondale
Magley
Preble
Decatur Hi-Way Airport

Kingsland
Tocsin
Decatur
Rivare

Peterson
Kekionga Park
H
LANCASTER
KIRKLAND
WASHINGTON
ST MARYS
Wren

Murray
Curryville
Elm Tree Crossroads

Deam Oak
Craigville
Baltzell-Lenhart Woods Nature Preserve
Pleasant Mills

North Oaks
Honduras

1" = 2.5 mi (3.9 km)

Continue on Page 35

©DeLorme

Continue in DeLorme's Ohio Atlas & Gazetteer

29

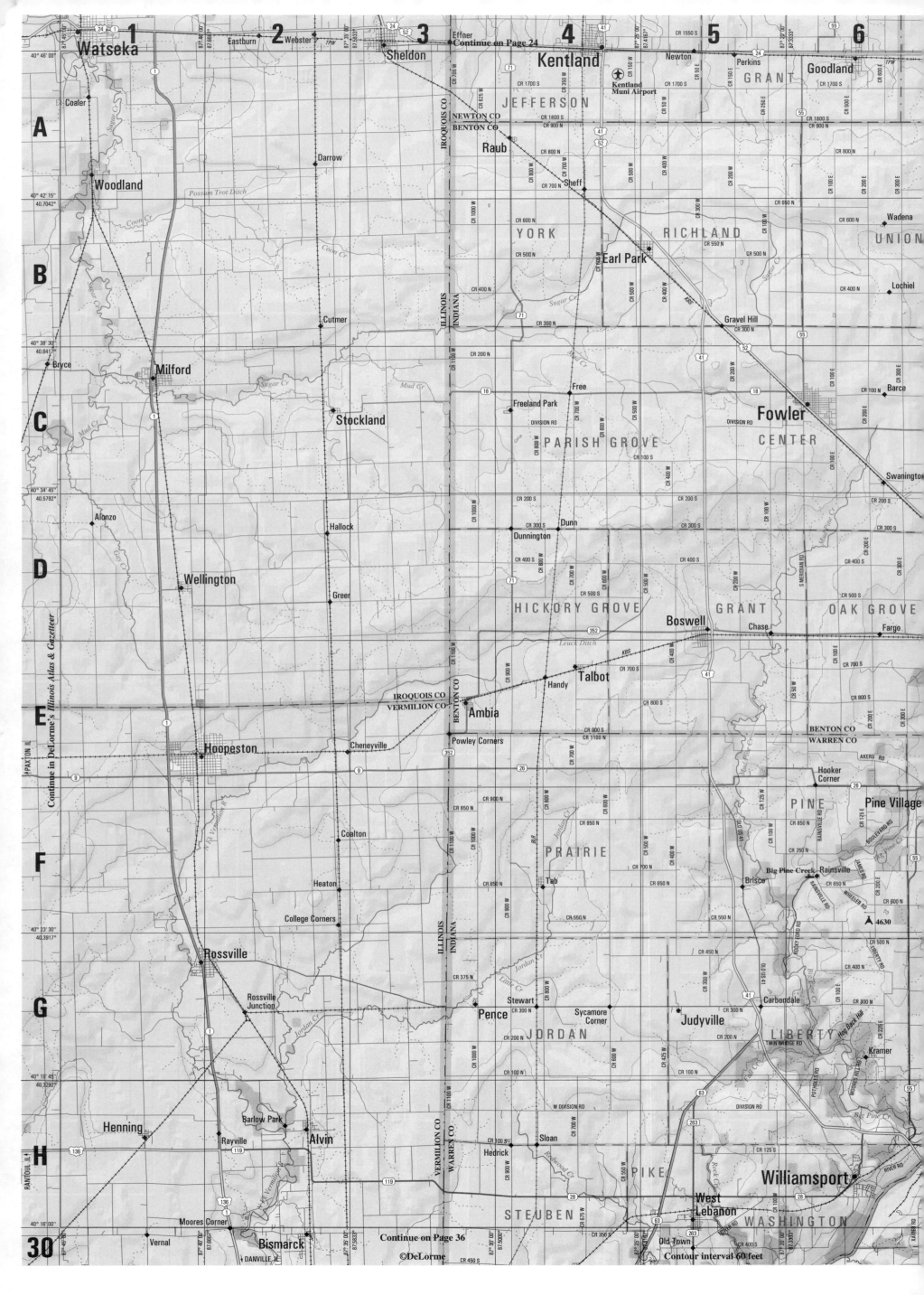

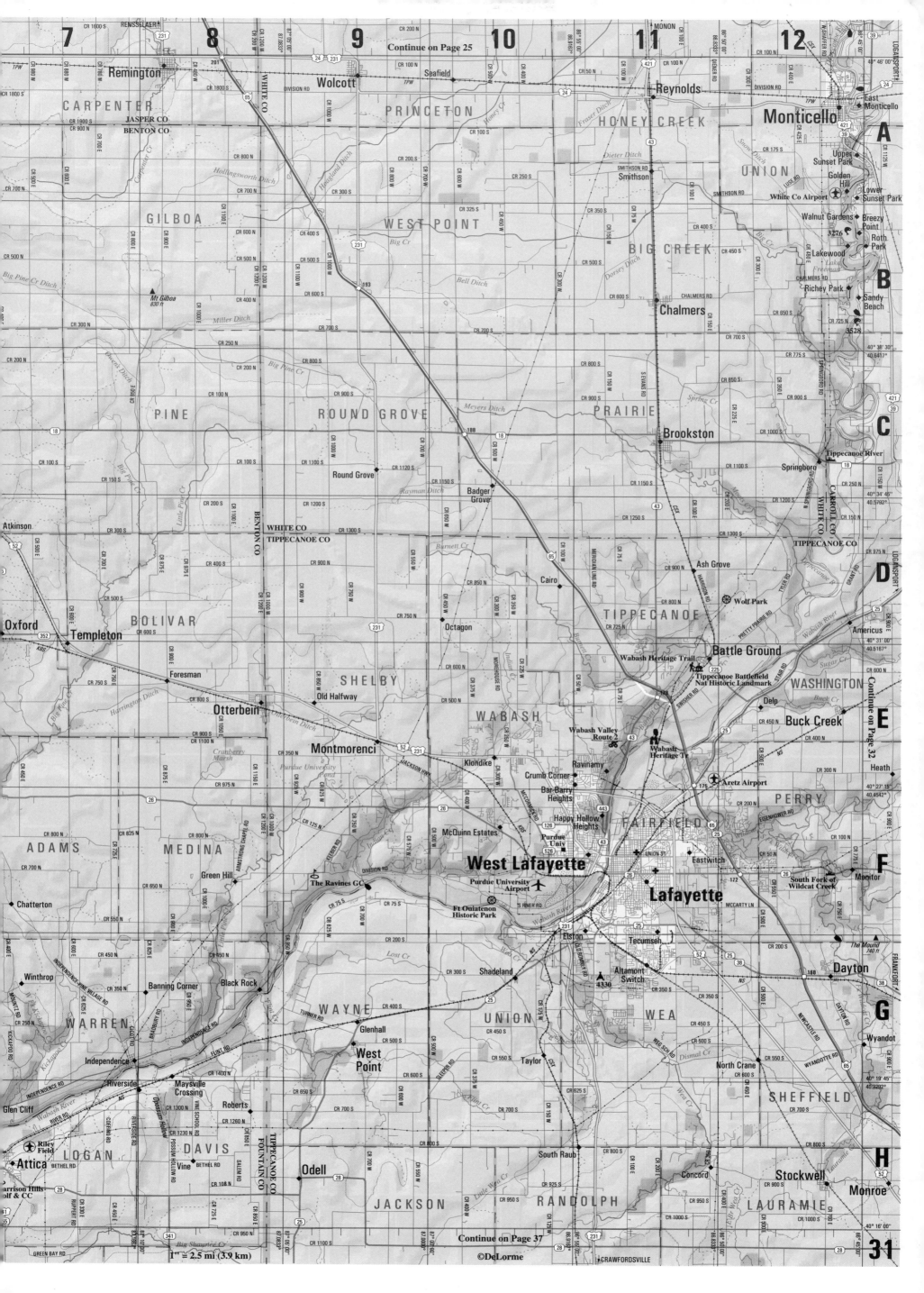

Continue on Page 25

Continue on Page 32

Continue on Page 37

1" = 2.5 mi (3.9 km)

©DeLorme

31

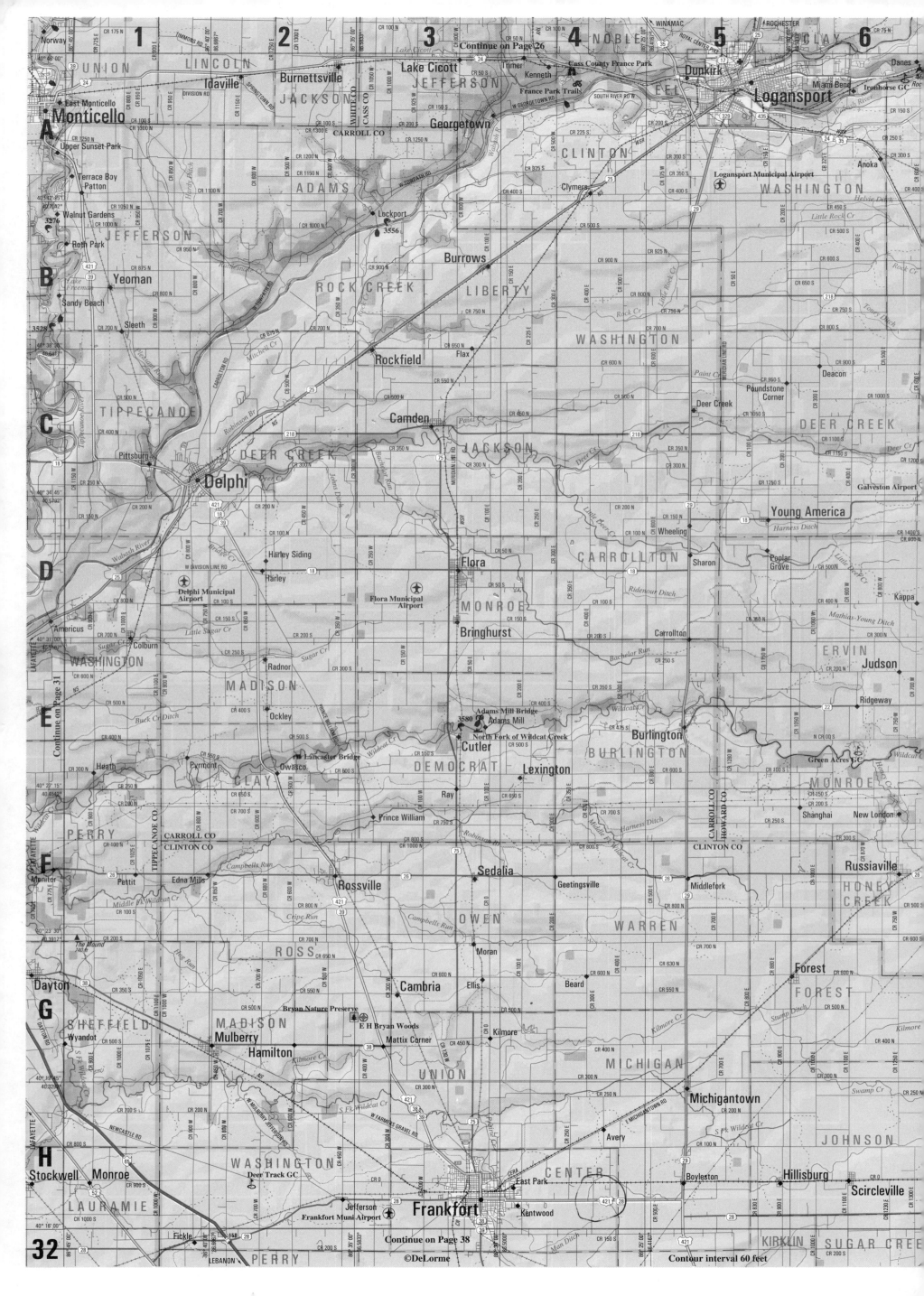

Continue on Page 27

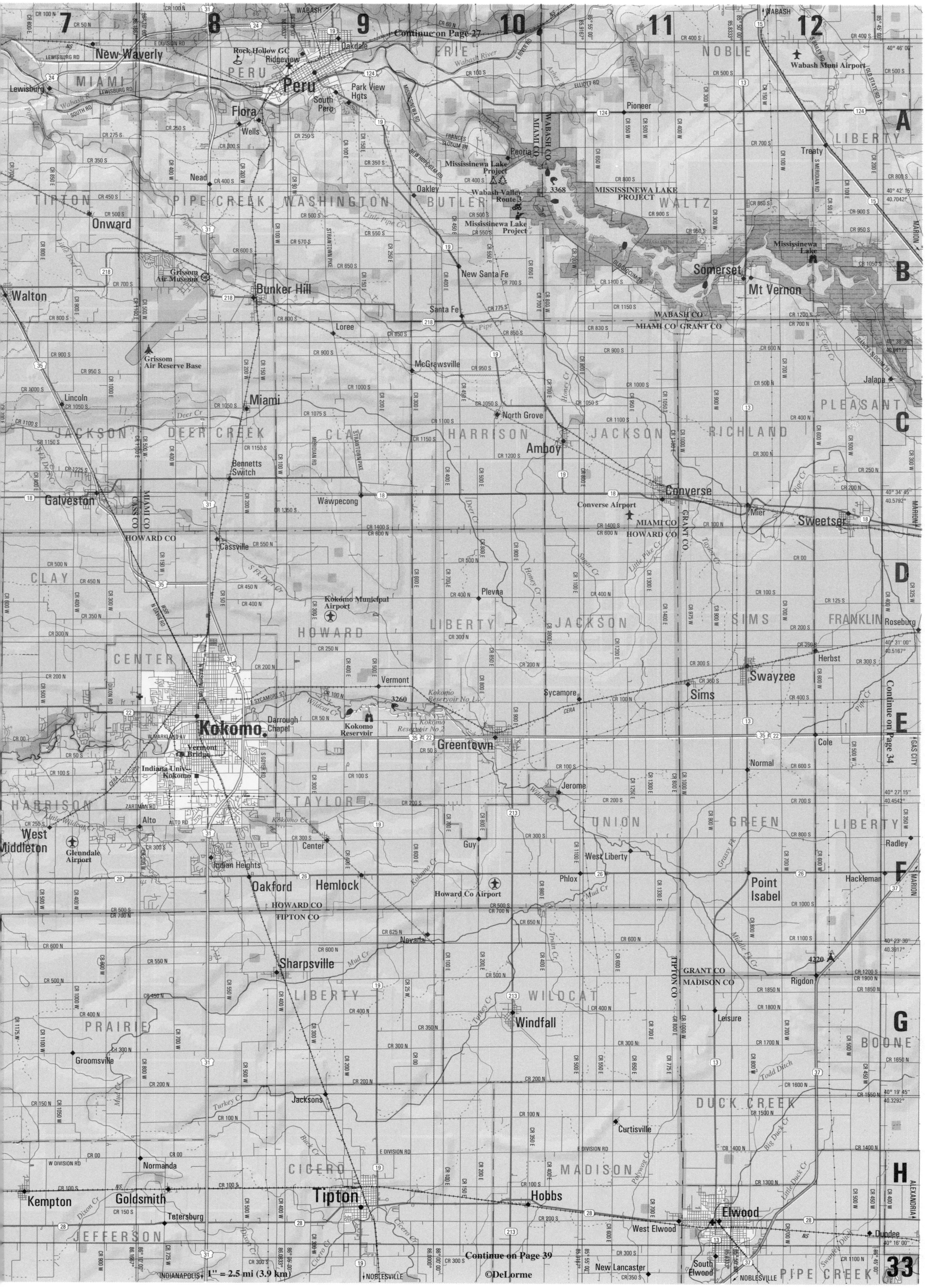

New Waverly
Lewisburg
MIAMI
PERU
Peru
Rock Hollow GC
Ridgeview
Oakdale
Wabash River
ERIE
NOBLE
Wabash Muni Airport
LIBERTY

Flora
Wells
South Peru
Park View Hgts
Pioneer
WABASH CO
MIAMI CO
Treaty

A

Nead
Peoria
Oakley
Mississinewa Lake Project
Wabash Valley Route 3
3368
MISSISSINEWA LAKE PROJECT
WALTZ

Onward
TIPTON
PIPE CREEK
WASHINGTON
BUTLER
New Santa Fe
Mississinewa Lake Project
Somerset
Mt Vernon
Mississinewa Lake

B

Walton
Grissom Air Museum
Bunker Hill
Santa Fe
Loree
Pipe
WABASH CO
MIAMI CO   GRANT CO
Jalapa

Grissom Air Reserve Base
McGrawsville
North Grove
PLEASANT

C

Lincoln
Miami
DEER CREEK
CLAY
HARRISON
Amboy
JACKSON
RICHLAND
Galveston
JACKSON
Bennetts Switch
Wawpecong
Converse Airport
Converse
Mier
Sweetser

CASS CO
HOWARD CO
Cassville
Plevna
MIAMI CO
HOWARD CO
GRANT CO

D

CLAY
Kokomo Municipal Airport
LIBERTY
JACKSON
SIMS
FRANKLIN
Roseburg
Herbst

CENTER
HOWARD
Vermont
3260
Kokomo Reservoir No 1
Sycamore
Sims
Swayzee

Kokomo
Darrough Chapel
Kokomo Reservoir
Kokomo Reservoir No 2
Greentown
Jerome
Normal
Cole

E

Indiana Univ Kokomo
Alto
Center
Guy
UNION
GREEN
LIBERTY
Radley

HARRISON
West Middleton
Glenndale Airport
Indian Heights
Oakford
Hemlock
Howard Co Airport
West Liberty
Phlox
Point Isabel
Hackleman

F

HOWARD CO
TIPTON CO
Nevada
Sharpsville
LIBERTY
WILDCAT
GRANT CO
MADISON CO
4220
Rigdon

G

PRAIRIE
Groomsville
Jacksons
Windfall
Leisure
BOONE

Curtisville
DUCK CREEK

H

Kempton
Goldsmith
Tetersburg
Normanda
CICERO
Tipton
Hobbs
MADISON
Elwood
West Elwood
Alexandria

JEFFERSON
Dundee
South Elwood
New Lancaster
PIPE CREEK
NOBLESVILLE

33

INDIANAPOLIS 1" = 2.5 mi (3.9 km)

Continue on Page 39

Continue on Page 34

©DeLorme

Continue on Page 28

A   **B**   **C**   **D**   **E**   **F**   **G**   **H**

3452

Switchgrass Marshes   Salamonie Lake Project   Majenica Marsh   Majenica

HUNTINGTON   Rockford

Lincolnville   Lancaster   SALAMONIE LAKE PROJECT

LAGRO   POLK   LANCASTER   ROCK CREEK   ROCK CREEK

WABASH   Etna Acres GC   Mt Etna   Plum Tree   HUNTINGTON CO   WELLS CO

LIBERTY   WAYNE   JEFFERSON   SALAMONIE   LIBERTY   Liberty Center

Banquo   Pleasant Plain   Warren   Buckeye

La Fontaine   WABASH CO   HUNTINGTON CO   GRANT CO   Milo   Mt Zion

MISSISSINEWA LAKE PROJECT   Fox   Hart GC   McNatts   CHESTER

Jalapa   FRANCES SLOCUM TR   WASHINGTON   Landess   Van Buren   VAN BUREN   JACKSON   Jeff

PLEASANT   Shadeland   Hanfield   Dillman   Keystone

Sweetser   Farrville

Marion   Dooville   Friendly Corner   Roll   Montpelier   Matamoras

FRANKLIN   CENTER   Lake Wood   Arcana   Jadden   MONROE   WASHINGTON   HARRISON

Roseburg   Kiley   Home Corner   BLACKFORD CO   WELLS CO

Michaelsville   Brookhaven   Indiana Wesleyan Univ

Marion Municipal Airport   Gas City   Walnut Creek GCs   4600

Jonesboro   MILL   Upland   Renner   Hartford City

Weaver   Taylor Univ   4420

Radley   Laurel Lakes GC

LIBERTY   FAIRMOUNT   JEFFERSON   LICKING   JACKSON

Hackleman   Shamrock Lake   Millgrove

James Dean Gallery   Fairmount   Fowlerton

Matthews   Cumberland Bridge

GRANT CO   BLACKFORD CO   DELAWARE CO

Janney   Wheeling   UNION   Eaton

BOONE   VAN BUREN   WASHINGTON   NILES

Summitville   Stockport   Granville

Gaston   Shideler

MONROE   HARRISON   HAMILTON   DELAWARE

Orestes   Alexandria   Anthony   Mississinewa River   Royerton

Gimco City

Continue on Page 33   Continue on Page 40

©DeLorme

Contour interval 60 feet

Craigville

Continue on Page 29

FT WAYNE   Baltzell–Lenhart Woods Nature Preserve   FT WAYNE

Pleasant Mills

North Oaks

LANCASTER   KIRKLAND   WASHINGTON   ST MARYS

Toll Gate Heights

Honduras

Willshire

A

Bluffton

Coppess Corner   Monroe

VAN WERT CO / MERCER CO

Miller Airport

Ouabache SP

Salem

HARRISON   FRENCH   MONROE   BLUE CREEK

Travisville

Vera Cruz

B

Wellsburg

Poneto

Reiffsburg

Berne

Greenville

Linn Grove

Chattanooga

ADAMS CO / WELLS CO

WABASH   JEFFERSON

C

NOTTINGHAM   HARTFORD

Petroleum   Domestic

Ceylon Bridge   4010

Amishville USA
Ceylon

Nottingham   Phenix

Perryville

Geneva
Limberlost SHS

Rainbow Lake

Skeels Crossroads   Scudder

Jay City   New Corydon

JAY CO / BLACKFORD CO

Fiat

D

ADAMS CO / WELLS CO

Trinity

Wabash

MERCER CO / JAY CO

Balbec

Poling

Bryant
West Liberty

PENN   JACKSON   BEAR CREEK   WABASH

Twin Hills 1000 ft

Pennville

Kitt

Antiville

Westchester

E

Pleasant Ridge

Corkwell

Noble

Macedon

Trenton

St Peter

Ridertown

KNOX   GREENE   WAYNE   NOBLE

Pony   Center

Portland Municipal Airport

Bellfountain

St Joseph

F

Portland   Liber

Brice

Ft Recovery

Greene

College Corner

Converse

Blaine

Dunkirk   Como

Collett

Salamonia

G

RICHLAND   Redkey

New Mt Pleasant

Antioch

PIKE   MADISON

MERCER CO / DARKE CO

Powers

Bluff Point   Boundary City

JEFFERSON

4210

Salem

Bucks Corner

Albany   Fairview

New Pittsburg

JAY CO / RANDOLPH CO   RANDOLPH CO   JAY CO

H

GREEN

Ridgeville

Deerfield

WARD   JACKSON

Randolph

Cosmos

Brinckley
Davis–Purdue Agricultural Center Forest
1" = 2.5 mi (3.9 km)

Continue on Page 41

RICHMOND   UNION CITY   ©DeLorme

Continue on Page 30

Continue on Page 42

©DeLorme

Contour interval 60 feet

ATTICA LAFAYETTE

Continue on Page 31

LOGAN DAVIS JACKSON RANDOLPH LAURAMIE

FRANKFORT

Rob Roy Bridge
Rob Roy
Green Bay Rd
Aylesworth
Hunter Corner

Corwin Romney

TIPPECANOE CO
MONTGOMERY CO

Kirkpatrick

TIPPECANOE CO
MONTGOMERY CO

Newtown

RICHLAND

New Richmond

Linden

Continue on Page 31

Mellott

Wingate

COAL CREEK

MADISON

SUGAR CREEK

Graham

Stephens Crossing

Little Potato Cr

Simpson Corner

Elmdale

Cherry Grove

Darlington Woods

Hillsboro

Waynetown

Manchester

Darlington
Darlington Bridge

CAIN WAYNE

UNION

FRANKLIN

Wesley

Garfield

Smartsburg

Steam Corner

4080 Sugar Creek
Fiskville

Crawfordsville

Ben-Hur Museum
Wabash Coll

Ames

Taylor Corner

Yountsville

Mace

Wooley Corner

RIPLEY

Linnsburg

JACKSON

Hybernia

Wallace Bridge
Wallace

North Union

Whitesville

WALNUT

Alamo

Crawfordsville Muni Airport

New Market

Lake Holiday

SUGAR CREEK

FOUNTAIN CO
PARKE CO

Grange Corner

3512

Deers Mill Bridge Pine Hills

SHADES STATE PARK

Shades SP Trails
Pine Hills Nature Pres
Shades SP
Shades State Park Airport
Wabash Valley Route 1

Indian Cr

SCOTT CLARK

Ladoga

HOWARD

Byron

BROWN

Lapland

Wilkens Mill Bridge
TURKEY RUN SP
Rocky Hollow-Falls Canyon Nature Pres

Rocky Hollow-Falls Canyon

Narrows Bridge

3324

Browns Valley

Parkersburg

MONTGOMERY CO
PUTNAM CO

Cox Ford Bridge
Turkey Run SP

Lake Waveland

Waveland

Russellville

Raccoon

Cornstalk Bridge

Portland Mills Bridge

Roachdale

Marshall

Guion

Milligan

GREENE

RUSSELL

FRANKLIN

JACKSON

Bloomingdale

WASHINGTON

Judson

Fincastle

Carpentersville

PUTNAM CO
PARKE CO

Nyesville

Pine Bluff Bridge
New Maysville

3440 Terre Vin Winery

Rockville

Beeson Bridge
Billie Creek Bridge
Leatherwood Station Bridge
State Sanitorium Bridge
Bellmore

Portland Mills

CLINTON MONROE FLOYD

Rollingstone Bridge

Bainbridge

Hall Woods Nature Pres

erbridge Driving Tour
TERRE HAUTE

Billie Creek Village

UNION Hollandsburg

Continue on Page 43

BRAZIL GREENCASTLE

1" = 2.5 mi (3.9 km)

©DeLorme

Continue on Page 38

INDIANAPOLIS
LEBANON
DANVILLE

A B C D E F G H

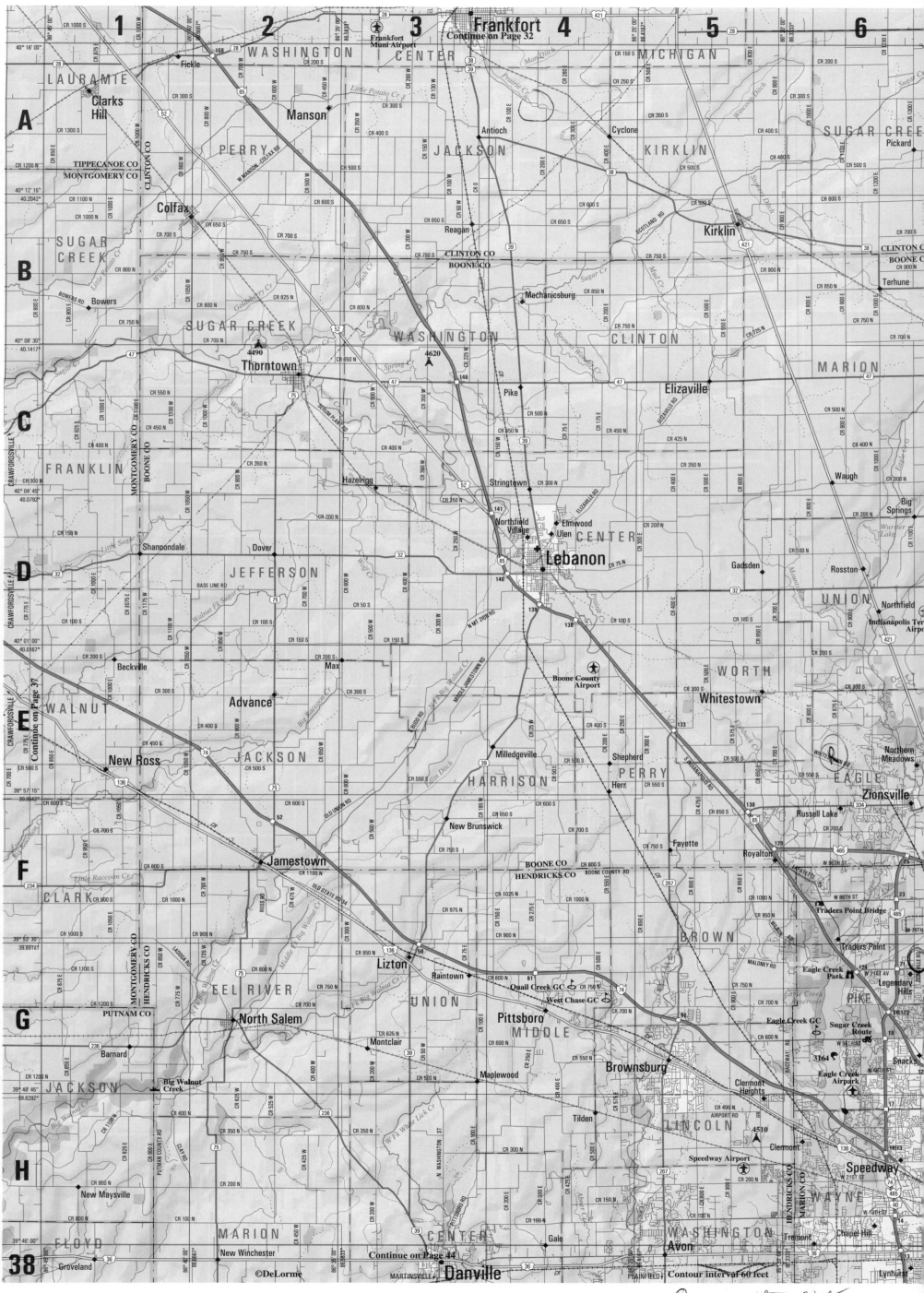

Continue on Page 32

Continue on Page 37

Continue on Page 44

38

©DeLorme

Contour interval 60 feet

O = geographic center of State

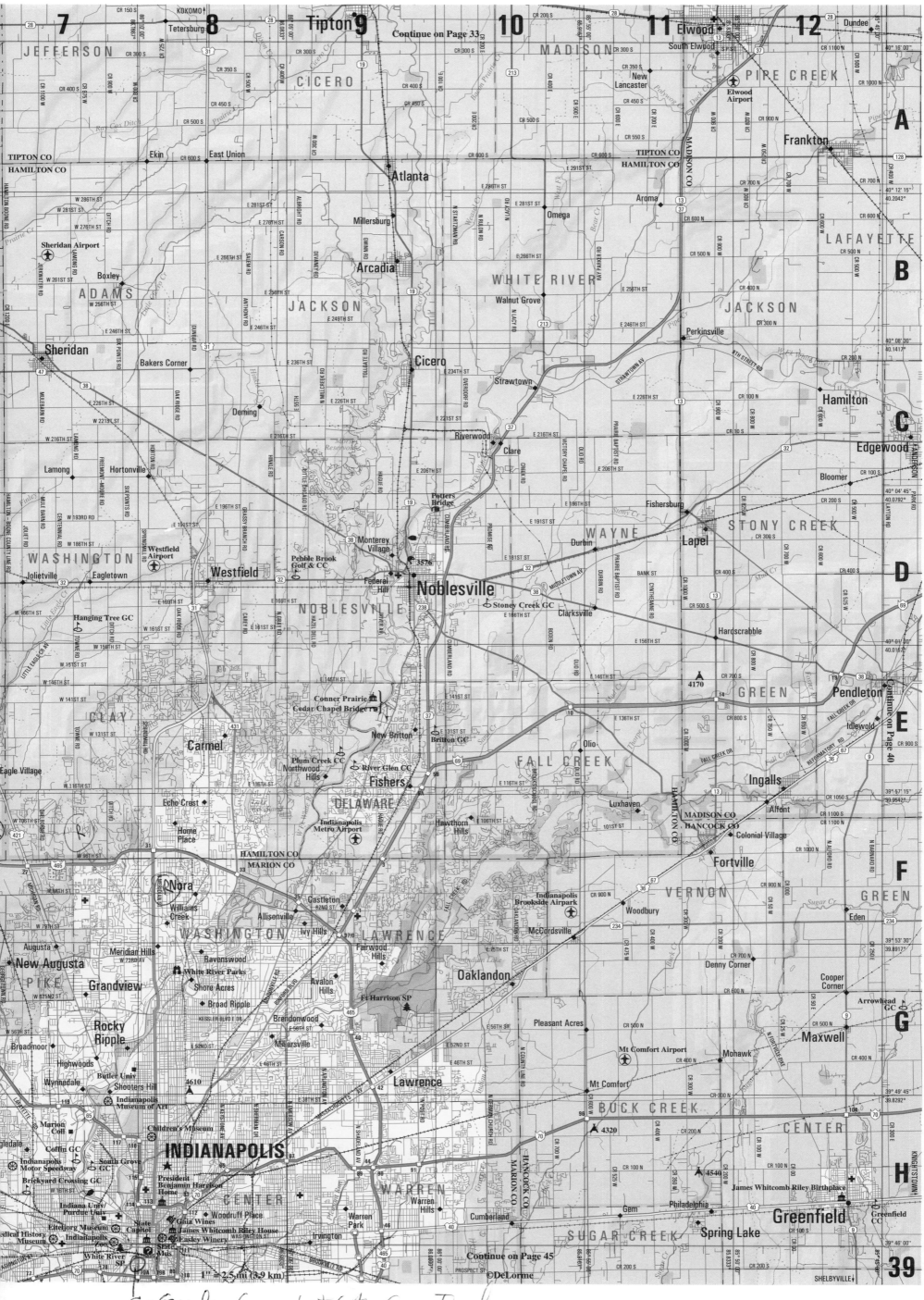

Continue on Page 33

Continue on Page 40

Continue on Page 45

©DeLorme

1" = 2.5 mi (3.9 km)

39

SHELBYVILLE

C = Greenlawn Cem - 1st City Cem Index

Continue on Page 34

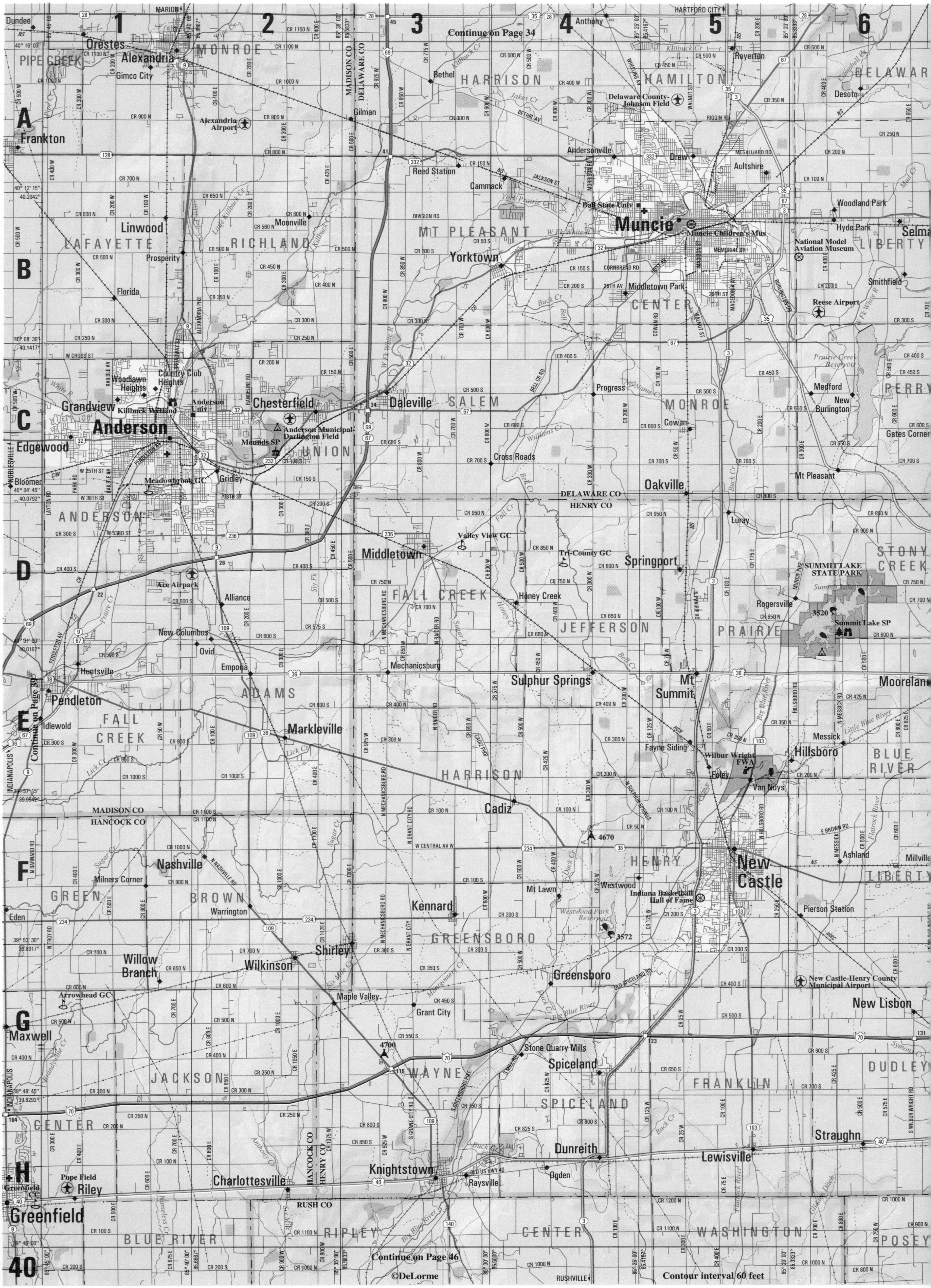

A

Dundee
Orestes
Alexandria
Gimco City
MONROE
Frankton
HARRISON
HAMILTON
DELAWARE
Royerton
Delaware County-Johnson Field
Desoto

B

PIPE CREEK
Bethel
Anthony
HARTFORD CITY
Reed Station
Cammack
Andersonville
Drew
Aultshire
Woodland Park
Hyde Park
Selma
Linwood
LAFAYETTE
RICHLAND
MT PLEASANT
Yorktown
Muncie
Ball State Univ
Muncie Children's Mus
National Model Aviation Museum
LIBERTY
Prosperity
Florida
Moonville
Gilman
CENTER
Middletown Park
Reese Airport
Smithfield

C

Grandview
Anderson
Killbuck Wetland
Anderson Univ
Woodlawn Heights
Country Club Heights
Chesterfield
Daleville
SALEM
Progress
MONROE
Medford
New Burlington
PERRY
Edgewood
Bloomer
Mounds SP
Anderson Municipal-Darlington Field
UNION
Cowan
Gates Corner
Mt Pleasant

D

ANDERSON
Meadowbrook GC
Gridley
Cross Roads
Oakville
DELAWARE CO
HENRY CO
Luray
STONY CREEK
Valley View GC
Middletown
Tri-County GC
Springport
SUMMIT LAKE STATE PARK
Ace Airpark
Alliance
FALL CREEK
Honey Creek
JEFFERSON
PRAIRIE
Rogersville
3520
Summit Lake SP
New Columbus
Ovid
Emporia
Mechanicsburg
Sulphur Springs
Mt Summit
Mooreland

E

Huntsville
Pendleton
Idlewold
FALL CREEK
Markleville
ADAMS
HARRISON
Cadiz
Fayne Siding
Messick
Wilbur Wright FWA
Hillsboro
BLUE RIVER
Foley
Van Nuys

F

MADISON CO
HANCOCK CO
Nashville
Milners Corner
GREEN
BROWN
Warrington
Kennard
4670
HENRY
New Castle
Mt Lawn
Westwood
Indiana Basketball Hall of Fame
LIBERTY
Millville
Ashland
Pierson Station

G

Eden
Willow Branch
Wilkinson
Shirley
Maple Valley
Grant City
GREENSBORO
Greensboro
3572
Westwood Park Reservoir
New Castle-Henry County Municipal Airport
New Lisbon
Arrowhead GC
Maxwell
4700
Stone Quarry Mills
Spiceland
FRANKLIN
Straughn
DUDLEY

H

Greenfield CC
Pope Field
Riley
Greenfield
JACKSON
CENTER
Charlottesville
RUSH CO
Knightstown
Raysville
Ogden
Dunreith
Lewisville
WAYNE
SPICELAND
Symons
Pope Field
BLUE RIVER
RIPLEY
CENTER
WASHINGTON
POSEY

Continue on Page 46

©DeLorme

Contour interval 60 feet

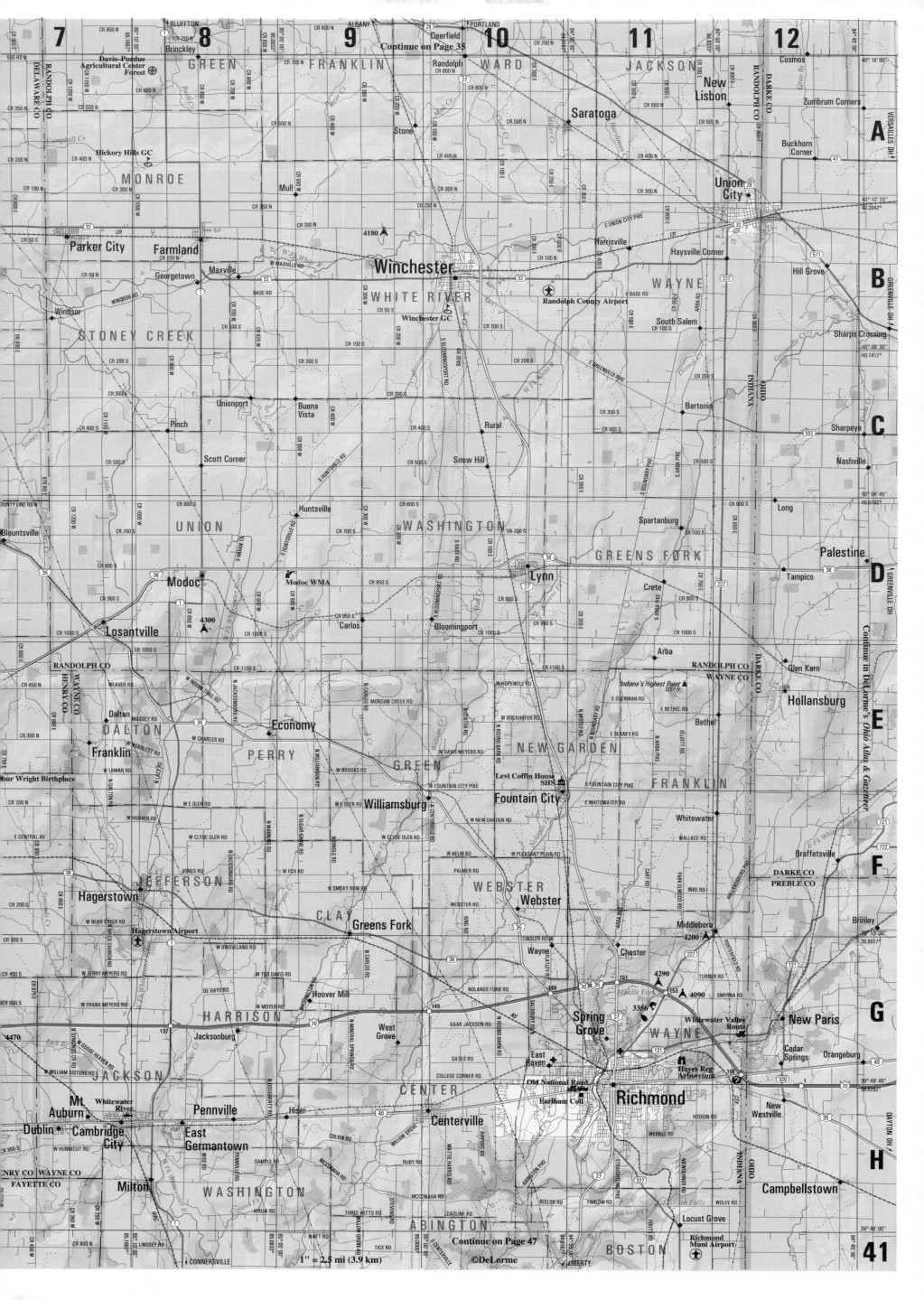

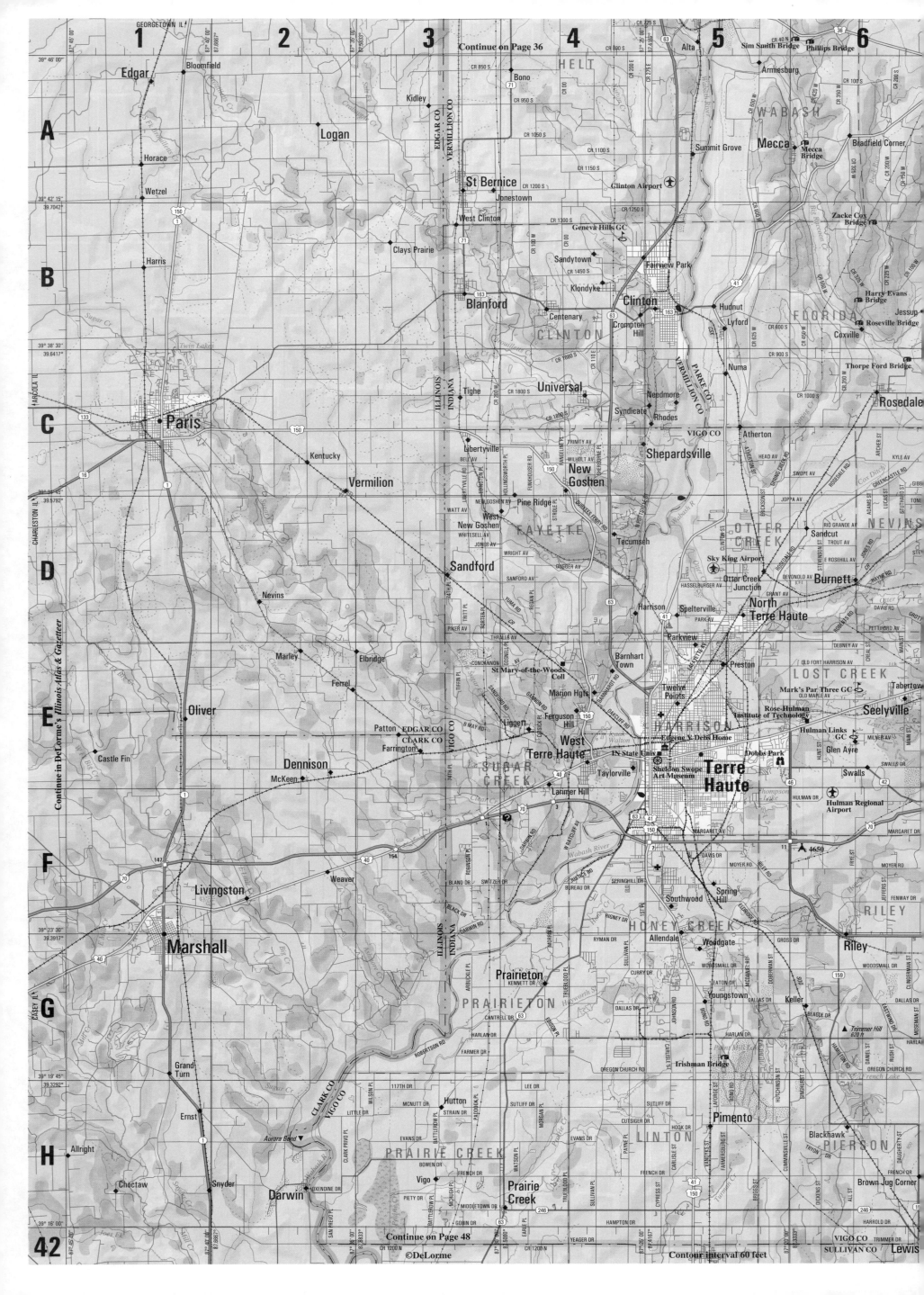

Continue on Page 36

1 **2** **3** **4** **5** **6**

A

B

C

D

E

F

G

H

42

©DeLorme

Continue on Page 48

Contour interval 60 feet

GEORGETOWN IL

Edgar
Bloomfield
Horace
Wetzel
Harris

Logan
Kidley
St Bernice
Jonestown
West Clinton
Clays Prairie
Blanford
Centenary
Crompton Hill

Paris
Kentucky
Vermilion
Sandford
Nevins
Marley
Elbridge
Ferrel
Oliver
Castle Fin
Dennison
McKeen

Patton
Farrington
EDGAR CO
CLARK CO

Livingston
Weaver
Marshall
Grand Turn
Ernst
Allright
Choctaw
Snyder
Darwin
Aurora Bend

Bono
HELT
Alta
Sim Smith Bridge
Phillips Bridge
Armesburg
WABASH
Mecca
Mecca Bridge
Bradfield Corner
Summit Grove
Clinton Airport
Sandytown
Klondyke
Fairview Park
Clinton
Hudnut
Lyford
Harry Evans Bridge
Jessup
FLORIDA
Roseville Bridge
Coxville
Zacke Cox Bridge
CLINTON
Geneva Hills GC
Numa
Thorpe Ford Bridge
Tighe
Universal
Needmore
Syndicate
Rhodes
VIGO CO
Atherton
Rosedale
Libertyville
Trinity AV
New Goshen
Shepardsville
New Goshen
Pine Ridge
FAYETTE
Tecumseh
OTTER CREEK
Sandcut
NEVINS
Rio Grande
Sky King Airport
Otter Creek Junction
Burnett
Harrison
Spelterville
North Terre Haute
Parkview
Preston
LOST CREEK
Tabertown
St Mary-of-the-Woods Coll
Barnhart Town
Twelve Points
Mark's Par Three GC
Seelyville
Marion Hgts
Rose-Hulman Institute of Technology
Hulman Links GC
Glen Ayre
Ferguson Hill
Liggett
HARRISON
West Terre Haute
Eugene V. Debs Home
IN State Univ
Terre Haute
Dobbs Park
Swalls
Taylorville
Sheldon Swope Art Museum
Larimer Hill
Hulman Regional Airport
Weaver
Davis Dr
Southwood
Spring Hill
RILEY
HONEY CREEK
Allendale
Woodgate
Riley
Prairieton
PRAIRIETON
Youngstown
Keller
Trimmer Hill
Trishman Bridge
Hutton
Pimento
LINTON
PIERSON
Blackhawk
PRAIRIE CREEK
Vigo
Prairie Creek
Brown Jug Corner
VIGO CO
SULLIVAN CO
Lewis

ILLINOIS
INDIANA

EDGAR CO
VERMILLION CO

PARKE CO
VERMILLION CO

CLARK CO
VIGO CO

VIGO CO
SUGAR CREEK

Continue in DeLorme's Illinois Atlas & Gazetteer

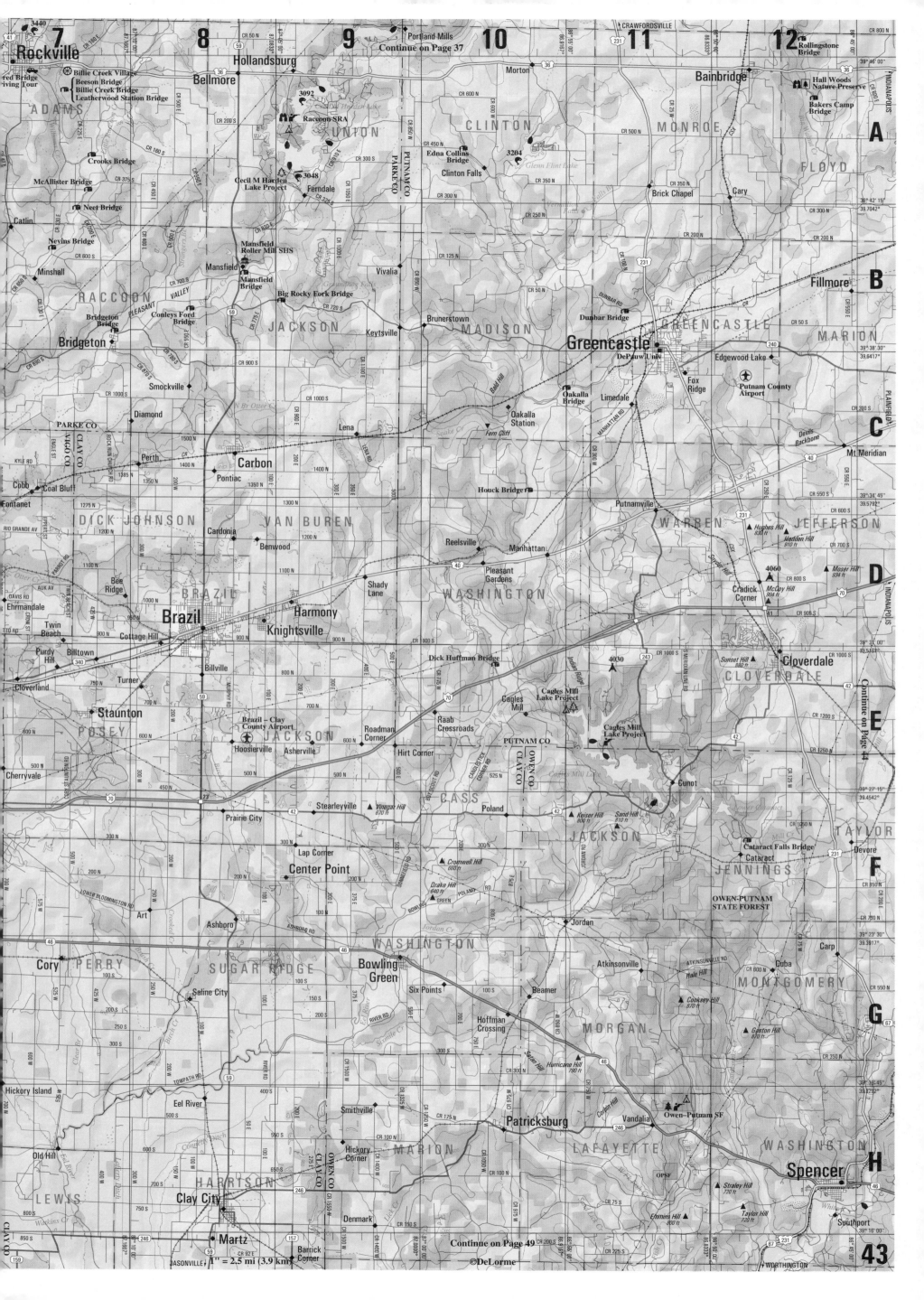

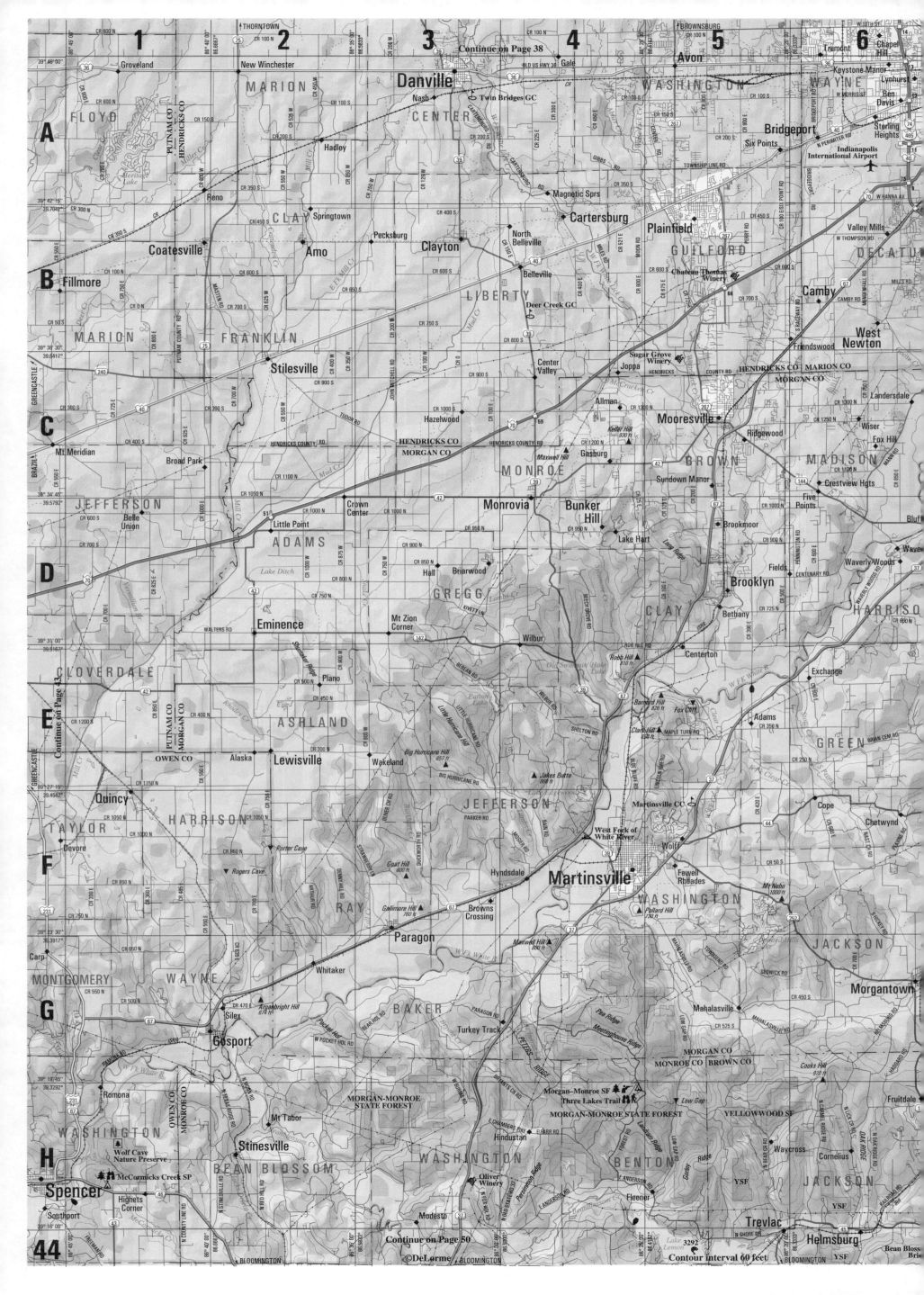

7 **8** **9** WARREN **10** **11** **12**

Medical History Museum
Indianapolis Zoo
State Capitol
Easley Winery
White River State Park
INDIANAPOLIS

Continue on Page 39

Spring Lake
CENTER
Gem
CR 100 S

Irvington
Post-Air Airport
Prospect St
Julietta
SUGAR CREEK
BRANDYWINE

Drexel Gardens
Maywood
Mars Hill
Beech Grove
Five Points
New Palestine
Reedville Station
Carrollton

University Hgts
Wanamaker
HANCOCK CO
SHELBY CO
Fountaintown

Rosedale Hills
Galader Station
FRANKLIN
Pleasant View
VAN BUREN
MORAL

Sunshine Gardens
Edgewood
Perry Manor
Acton
Sugar Creek
PERRY
Southport
Lindenwood
Brookfield
Green Meadows
London
Southeast Manor

Glenns Valley
Imperial Hills
Smock GC
Greenwood Muni Airport
MARION CO
JOHNSON CO
Sugar Creek
Clover Village

Smith Valley
Greenwood
Kelly Hall
Rocklane
Reds Corner
Fairland
MARION
Marion
Shelbyville Muni Airport

Hendricks
McGarty
Ville Vista CC
Frances
Critchfield
El Dorado
PLEASANT
CLARK
Rocklane Rd

WHITE RIVER
Walnut Ridge GC
SUGAR CREEK
BRANDYWINE
Boggstown
Candleglo Village
Hildebrand Village
Meiks

Travis Hill
Sally Daty Hill
Waterloo
Stones Crossing
ADDISON
Walkerville

Bluff Creek
Kinder
New Whiteland
Whiteland
Needham
Urmeyville
Shelbyville
Crestmoor
Riley Village

Bargersville
Old Bargersville
Donalds Knoll
Legends of Indiana GC
HENDRICKS
McCrea Hill
SHELBY

Providence
Hopewell
Franklin
Franklin College of Indiana
NEEDHAM
Bengal
Smithland
Fenns
Marietta

Turkey Hill
UNION
FRANKLIN
Mt Pleasant
McFarren Hill
Wilson

Bud
Franklin Flying Field
Amity
Anita
Trafalgar
Samaria
Tameka Woods GC

NINEVEH
Lewis Creek
Camp Flat Rock
Flatrock River

BLUE RIVER
JACKSON
Mt Auburn
WASHINGTON

HENSLEY
ATTERBURY FISH AND WILDLIFE AREA
Old Camp Atterbury
Atterbury FWA
Driftwood River
Willow Park
Flat Rock
Norristown

Camp Atterbury Maneuver Training Center
JOHNSON CO
BROWN CO
Edinburgh
Pleasant View Village
SHELBY CO
BARTHOLOMEW CO

Nineveh
Princes Lakes
Spearsville
Peoga
St Louis Crossing
Old St Louis

NINEVEH
GERMAN
FLAT ROCK
HAW CREEK
Hope

CAMP ATTERBURY MANEUVER TRAINING CENTER
HAMBLEN
Taylorsville
Northcliff
Clifford
Nortonburg

UNION
Taggart
Gatesville
North Gate
Columbus Municipal Airport
CLAY

Continue on Page 51
Continue on Page 46

1" = 2.5 mi (3.9 km)
©DeLorme
COLUMBUS

45

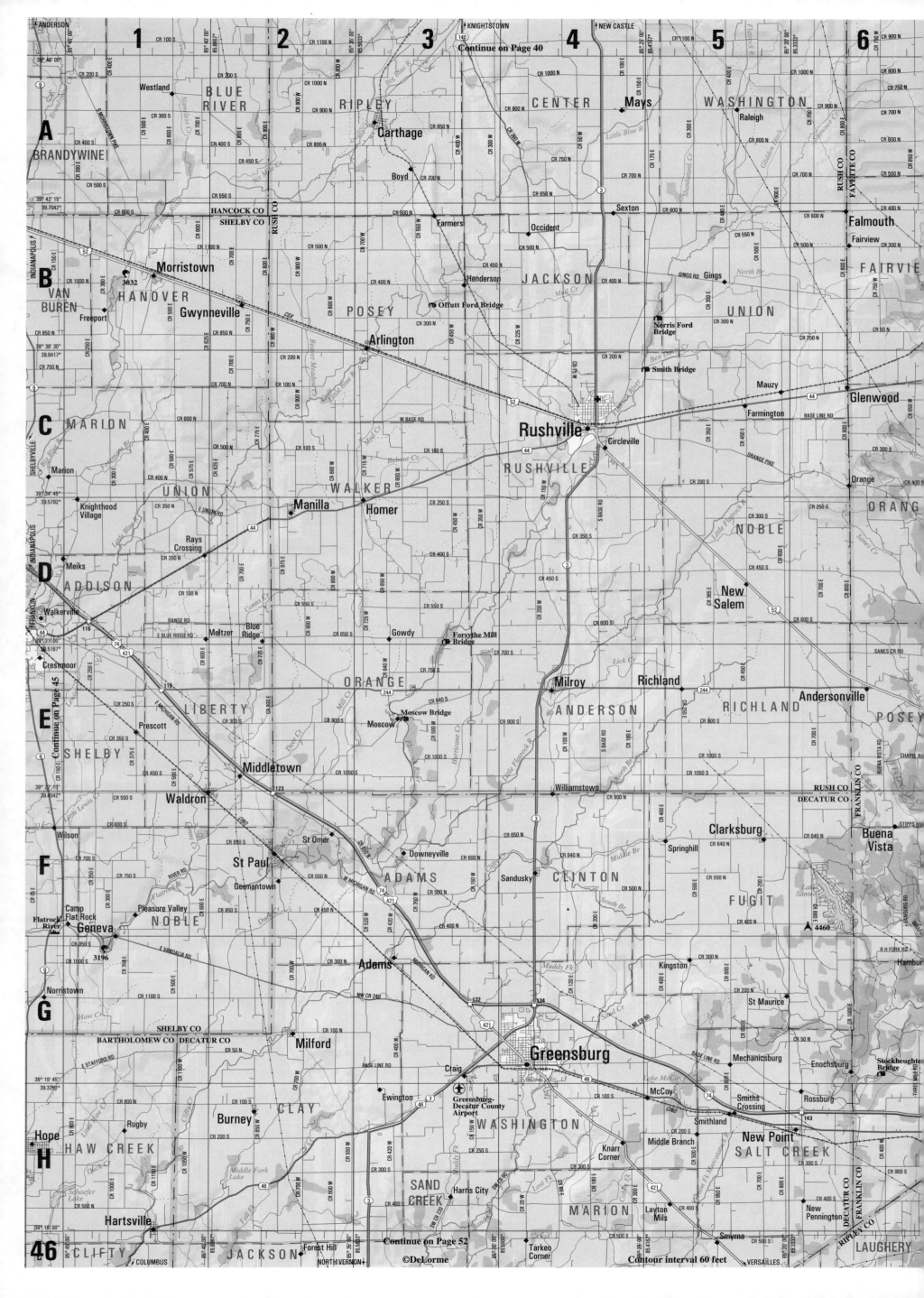

ANDERSON
KNIGHTSTOWN
NEW CASTLE

Continue on Page 40

A

Westland

BLUE
RIVER

RIPLEY

CENTER

Mays

WASHINGTON

Raleigh

BRANDYWINE

Carthage

Boyd

B

HANCOCK CO
SHELBY CO

Farmers

Occident

Sexton

Falmouth

Fairview

FAIRVIE

VAN
BUREN

Morristown

HANOVER

Henderson

JACKSON

Gings

Freeport

Gwynneville

Offutt Ford Bridge

UNION

Norris Ford
Bridge

Arlington

POSEY

Mauzy

C

Smith Bridge

Glenwood

MARION

Rushville

Farmington

Circleville

UNION

RUSHVILLE

Orange

Knighthood
Village

Manilla

Homer

WALKER

NOBLE

ORANG

D

Marion

Rays
Crossing

Meiks

New
Salem

ADDISON

Walkerville

Meltzer

Blue
Ridge

Gowdy

Forsythe Mill
Bridge

Crestmoor

ORANGE

Milroy

Richland

RICHLAND

Andersonville

POSE

E

LIBERTY

Moscow Bridge

Moscow

ANDERSON

Prescott

SHELBY

Middletown

Williamstown

RUSH CO
DECATUR CO

F

Waldron

Wilson

St Omer

Clarksburg

Buena
Vista

St Paul

Downeyville

Springhill

Germantown

ADAMS

Sandusky

CLINTON

FUGIT

Pleasure Valley

Camp
Flat Rock

NOBLE

G

Flatrock
River

Geneva

Adams

Kingston

Norristown

St Maurice

SHELBY CO
BARTHOLOMEW CO DECATUR CO

Milford

Greensburg

Mechanicsburg

Enochsburg

Stockheughter
Bridge

H

Craig

Burney

CLAY

Ewington

Greensburg-
Decatur County
Airport

WASHINGTON

McCoy

Smiths
Crossing

Rossburg

Hope

Rugby

Smithland

New Point

SALT CREEK

Hartsville

HAW CREEK

Knarr
Corner

Middle Branch

Harris City

SAND
CREEK

MARION

Layton
Mills

New
Pennington

Smyrna

CLIFTY

JACKSON

Forest Hill

NORTH VERNON

©DeLorme

Continue on Page 52

Tarkeo
Corner

VERSAILLES

LAUGHERY

Contour interval 60 feet

Continue on Page 45

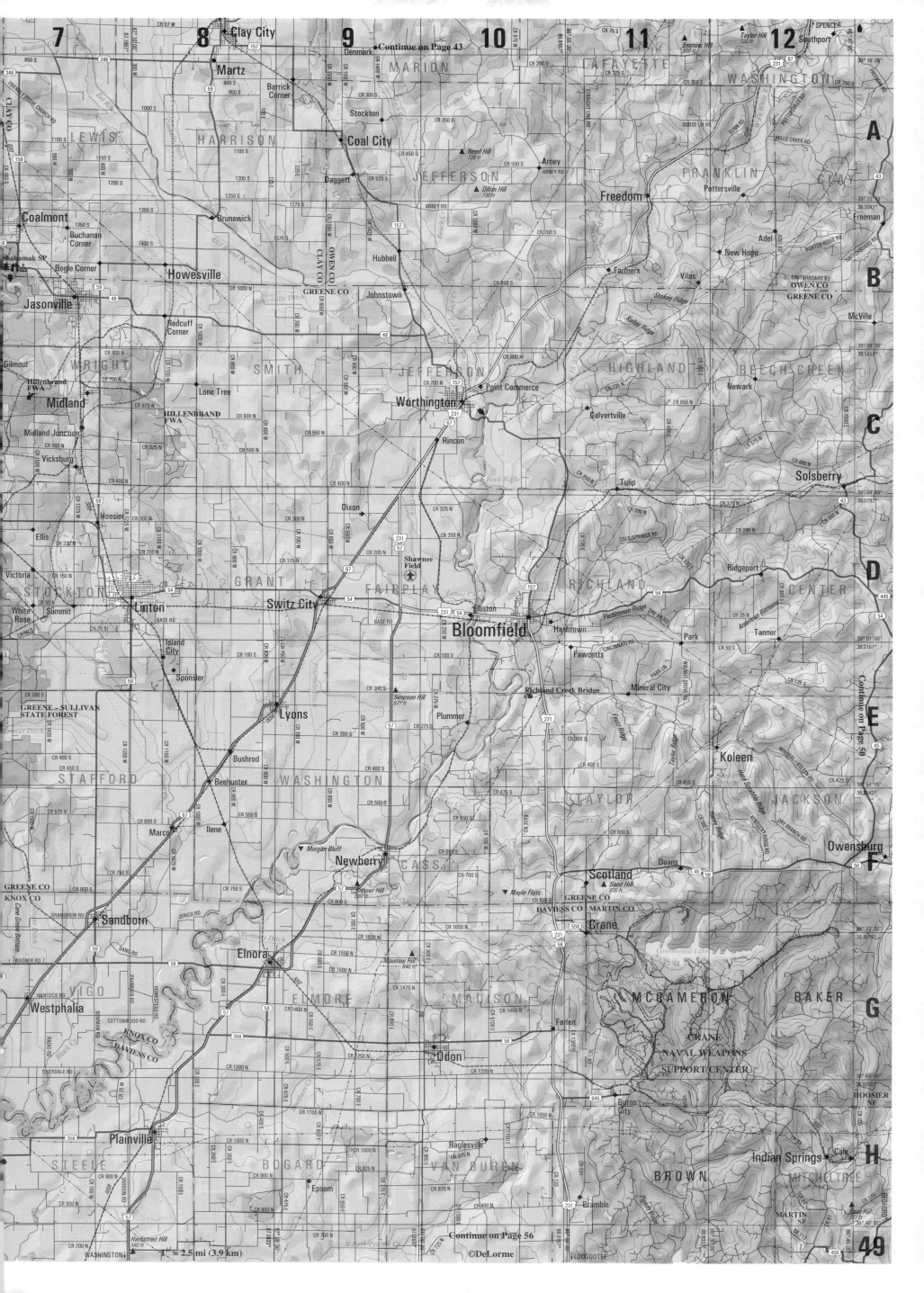

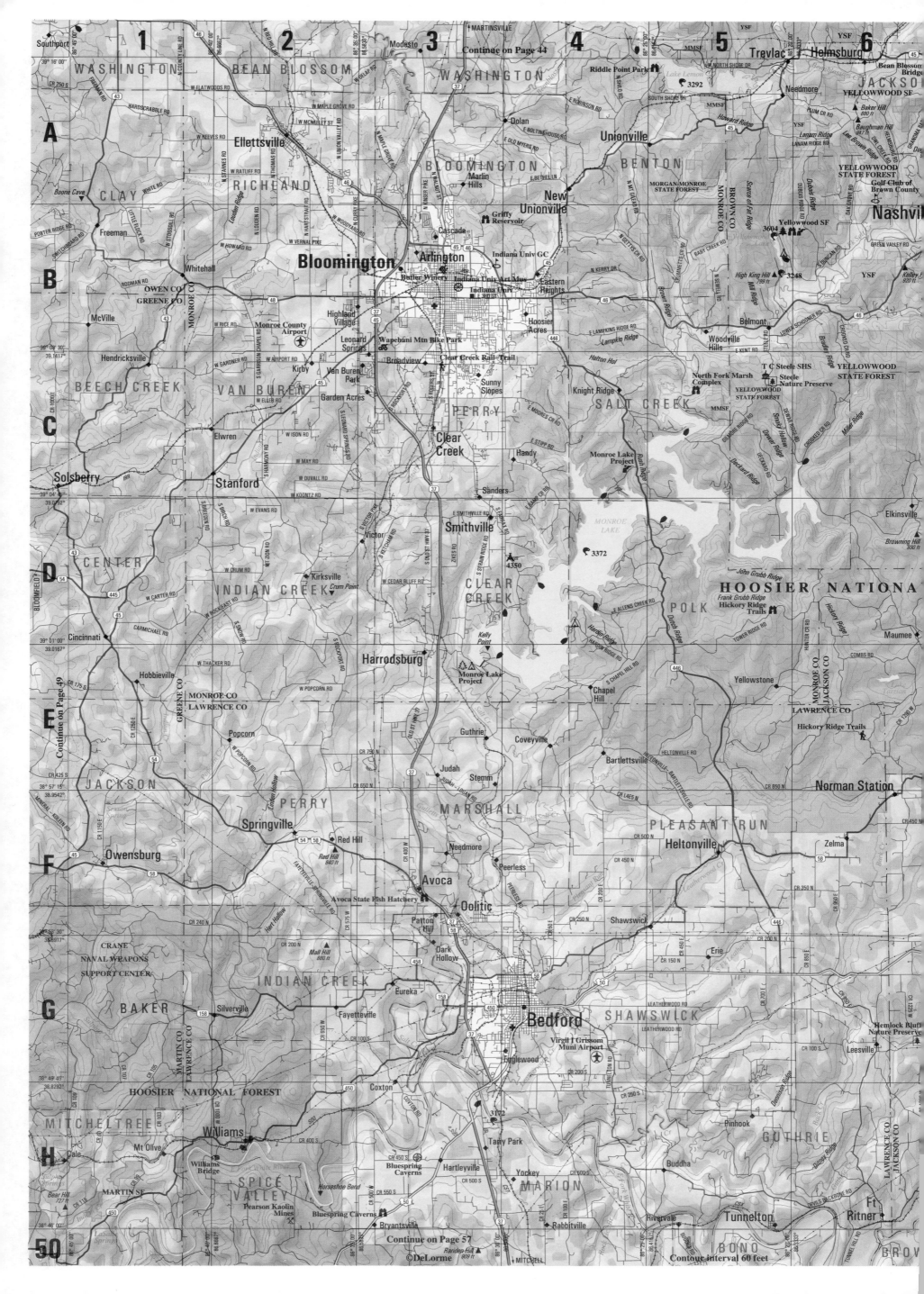

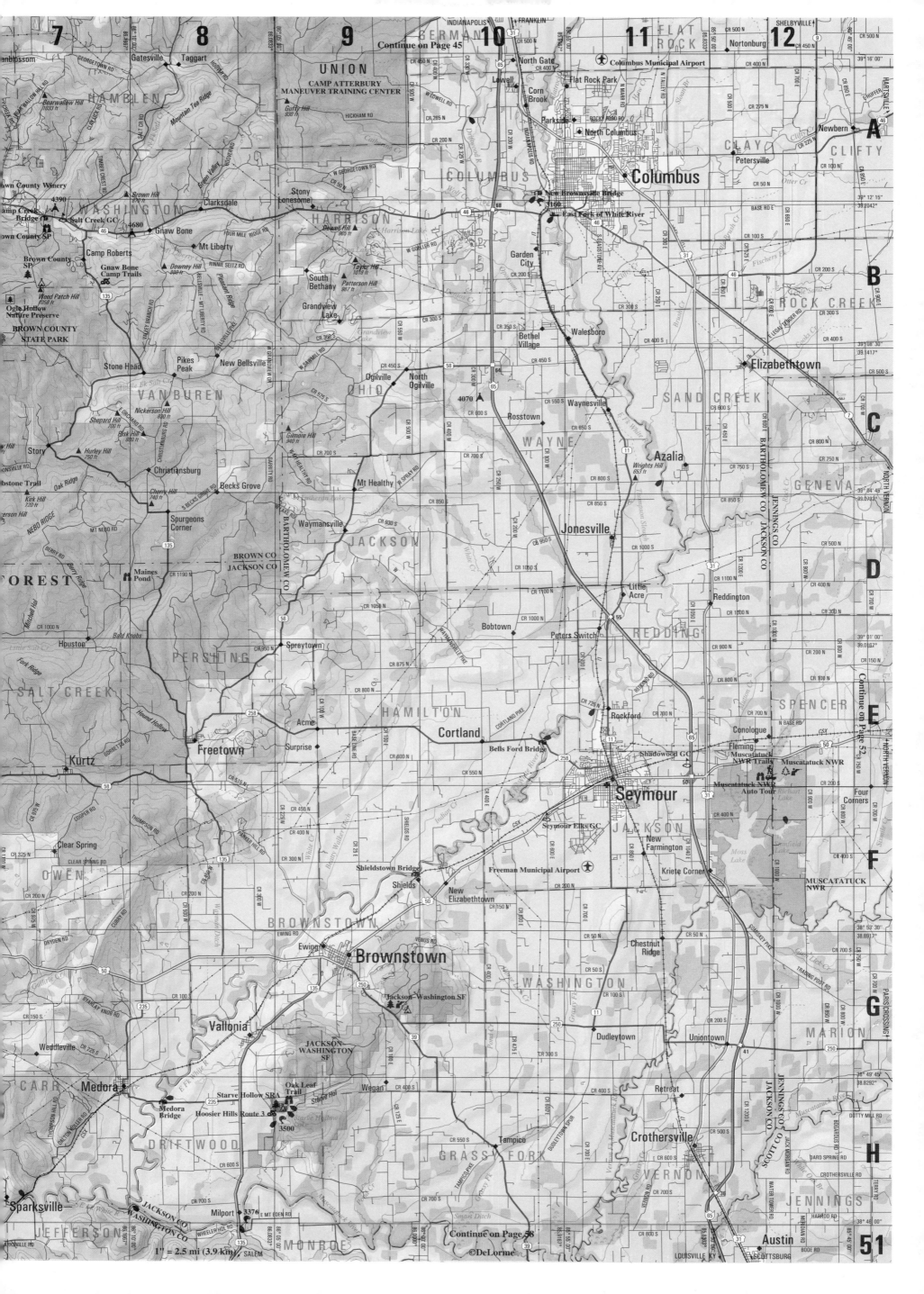

Continue on Page 45
Continue on Page 52
Continue on Page 58

1" = 2.5 mi (3.9 km)

©DeLorme

51

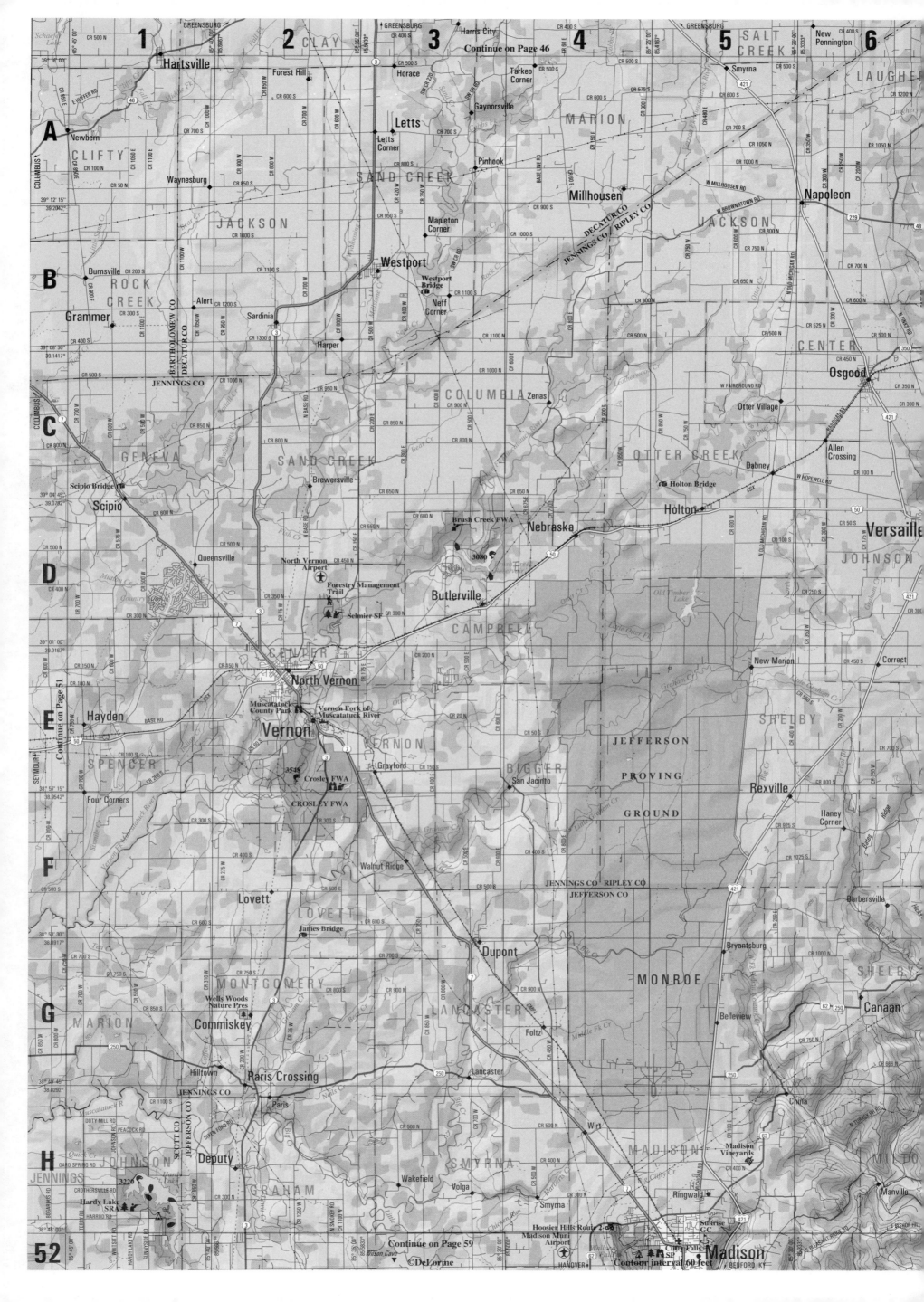

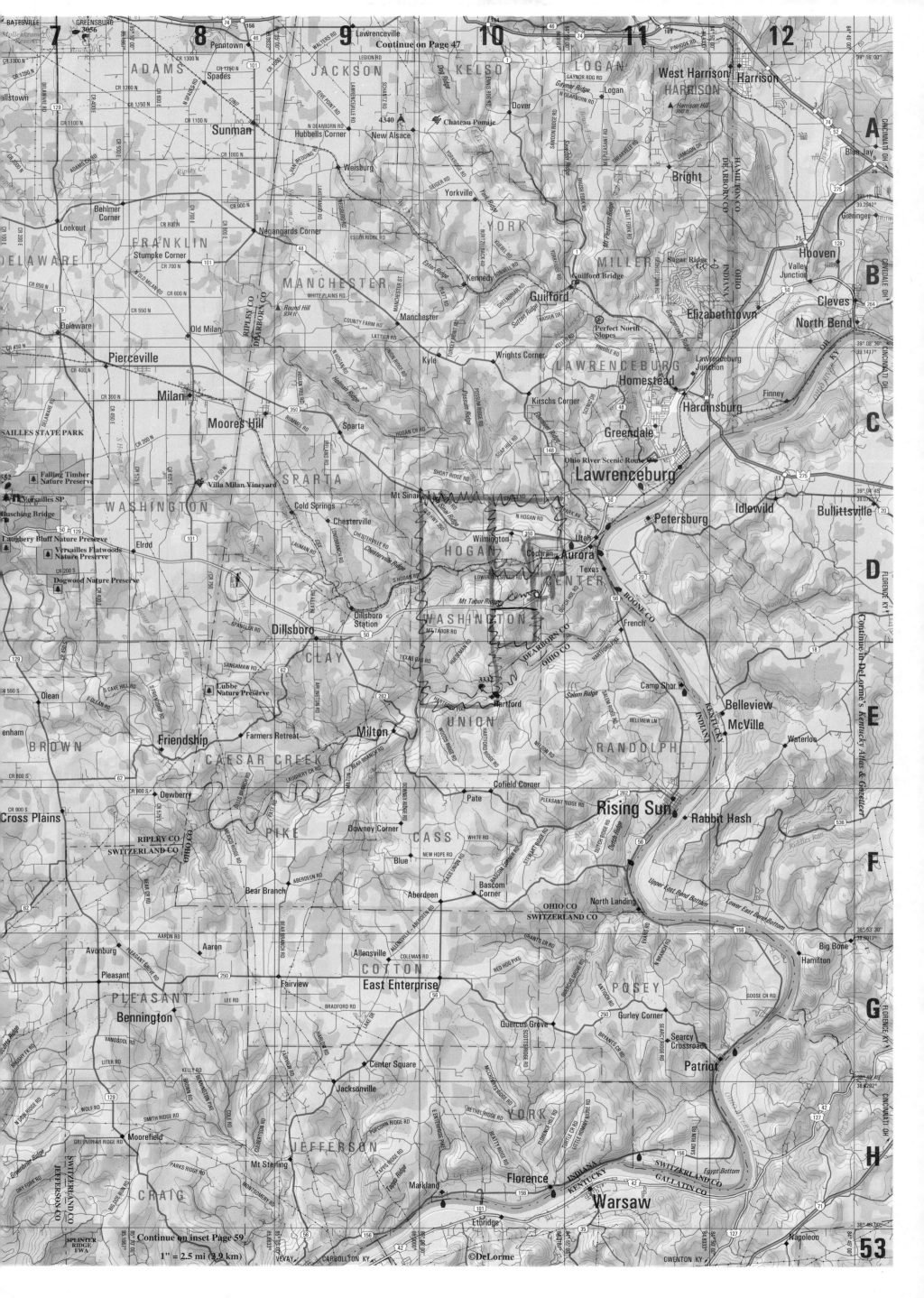

1 2 3 4 5 6

A

B

C

D

E

F

G

H

CHARLESTON IL↑

Continue in DeLorme's
Illinois Atlas & Gazetteer

88° 15' 00"
88° 10' 00"
88.1667°

38° 46' 00"

38° 42' 15"
38.7042°

38° 38' 30"
38.6417°

38° 34' 45"
38.5792°

38° 23' 30"
38.3917°

38° 19' 45"
38.3292°

38° 16' 00"

RICHLAND CO
LAWRENCE CO

87° 55' 00"
87.9167°

87° 50' 00"
87.8333°

Amity

Petrolia

Pureton

Olney

Claremont

Hadley

Sumner

Bridgeport

Red Hills Lake

Noble

CSX

Calhoun

Elbow

Schnell
38.6417°

Gallagher

Bonpas

Helena

Wynoose

RICHLAND CO
WAYNE CO

Berryville

Petersburg

Seminary

Parkersburg

RICHLAND CO / LAWRENCE CO
EDWARDS CO / WABASH CO

Lancaster

Maple Grove

Mesa Lake

Mt Erie

Bennington

West Salem

Friendsville

Samsville

Turkey Ridge

Black

Gards Point

Patto

Rattlesnake Bluff

Bone Gap

Odgen

Toms Prairie

Mt Carmel

Maud

Gibson Lake
Wildlife Habitat

EDWARDS CO
WABASH CO

Albion

Browns

Bellmont

Schrodts Station

Beech Bluff

Upper Drainage Ditch

Golden Gate

Ellery

Keensburg

Rochester

Skelton

Scottsville

Cowling

Crawleyville

Pearl Island

WABASH

Jimtown

Hickory Ridge

Continue on Page 60

©DeLorme

WAYNE CO / EDWARDS CO
WHITE CO

Grayville

CARMI IL↓

Contour interval 60 feet

Continue in DeLorme's *Illinois Atlas & Gazetteer*

MT VERNON IL

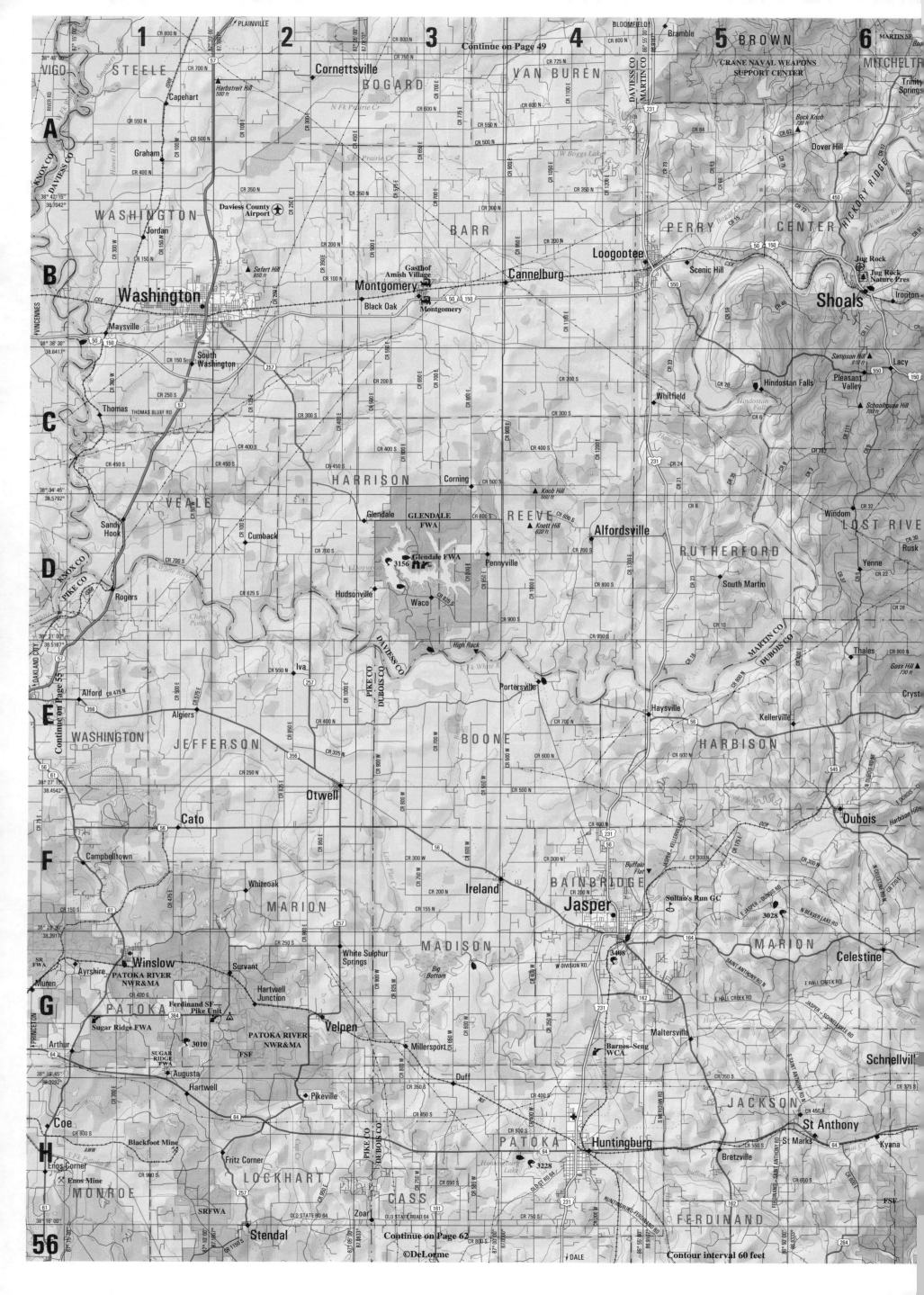

Continue on Page 49

Continue on Page 55

Continue on Page 62

©DeLorme

Contour interval 60 feet

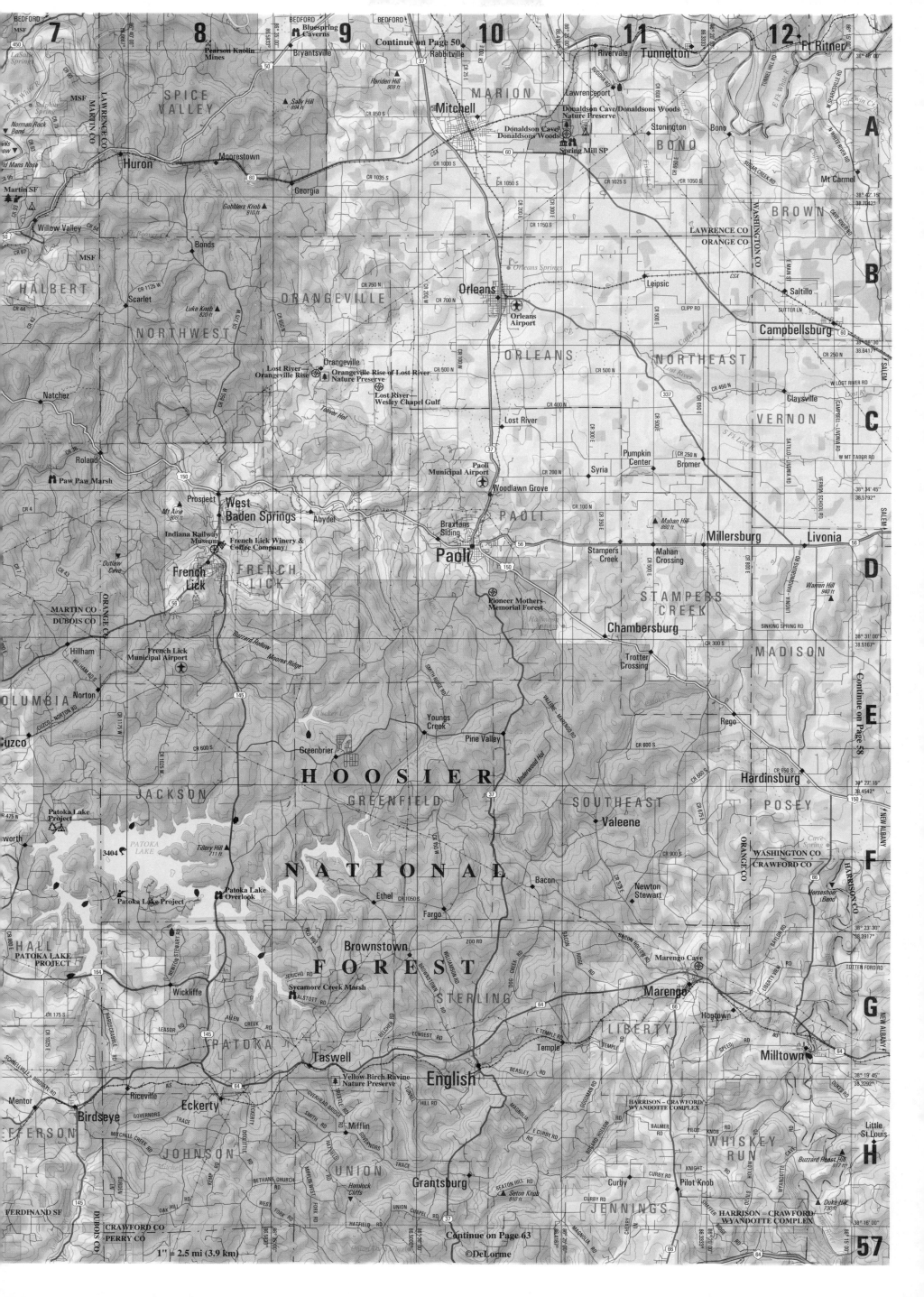

Continue on Page 50

Ft Ritner

MSF
450

BEDFORD
MSF

LaSalk
Spring

Pearson Kaolin
Mines

BEDFORD

Bluespring
Caverns

BEDFORD

Rivervale

Tunnelton

A

Norman Rock

Sulphur
Spring

SPICE
VALLEY

Bryantsville

Rabbitville

Rariden Hill
909 ft

MARION

Lawrenceport

Donaldson Cave/Donaldsons Woods
Nature Preserve

Stonington

Bono

Old Mans Nose

Huron

Moorestown

Sally Hill
894 ft

Mitchell

Donaldson Cave/
Donaldsons Woods

Spring Mill SP

BONO

Mt Carmel

Martin SF

Georgia

Gobblers Knob
910 ft

CR 1035 S

CR 1050 S

CR 1025 S

BROWN

Willow Valley

Bonds

LAWRENCE CO
ORANGE CO

B

HALBERT

Scarlet

Luke Knob
820 ft

ORANGEVILLE

Orleans Springs

Orleans

Leipsic

Saltillo

NORTHWEST

Orleans
Airport

NORTHEAST

Campbellsburg

Natchez

Orangeville

Lost River—
Orangeville Rise

Orangeville Rise of Lost River
Nature Preserve

ORLEANS

Claysville

C

Roland

Lost River—
Wesley Chapel Gulf

Lost River

Pumpkin
Center

Bromer

VERNON

Paw Paw Marsh

Paoli
Municipal Airport

Syria

Prospect

West
Baden Springs

Abydel

Woodlawn Grove

Mt Airie

Indiana Railway
Museum

French Lick Winery &
Coffee Company

Braxtons
Siding

PAOLI

Mahan Hill
860 ft

Millersburg

Livonia

D

French
Lick

FRENCH
LICK

Paoli

Stampers
Creek

Mahan
Crossing

Outlaw
Cave

MARTIN CO
DUBOIS CO

Pioneer Mothers
Memorial Forest

STAMPERS
CREEK

Warren Hill
940 ft

Hillham

French Lick
Municipal Airport

Chambersburg

MADISON

E

COLUMBIA

Norton

Buzzard Hollow

Moores Ridge

Youngs
Creek

Pine Valley

Rego

Cuzco

Greenbrier

HOOSIER

Hardinsburg

Patoka Lake
Project

3404

JACKSON

GREENFIELD

SOUTHEAST

POSEY

F

PATOKA
LAKE

Tillery Hill
711 ft

NATIONAL

Valeene

Cave
Spring

worth

Patoka Lake
Overlook

Patoka Lake Project

Bacon

WASHINGTON CO
CRAWFORD CO

Ethel

Newton
Stewart

Horseshoe
Bend

Fargo

ORANGE CO

HALL
PATOKA LAKE
PROJECT

FOREST

Brownstown

Marengo Cave

G

Wickliffe

Sycamore Creek Marsh

Halstott

STERLING

Marengo

Hogtown

LIBERTY

Milltown

Taswell

Yellow Birch Ravine
Nature Preserve

English

Temple

Mentor

Riceville

Eckerty

HARRISON–CRAWFORD
WYANDOTTE COMPLEX

Little
St Louis

H

Birdseye

Mifflin

WHISKEY
RUN

JEFFERSON

JOHNSON

UNION

Grantsburg

Hemlock
Cliffs

Seton Knob
610 ft

Curby

Pilot Knob

FERDINAND SF

CRAWFORD CO
PERRY CO

JENNINGS

HARRISON–CRAWFORD
WYANDOTTE COMPLEX

Continue on Page 63

1" = 2.5 mi (3.9 km)

©DeLorme

57

Continue on Page 58

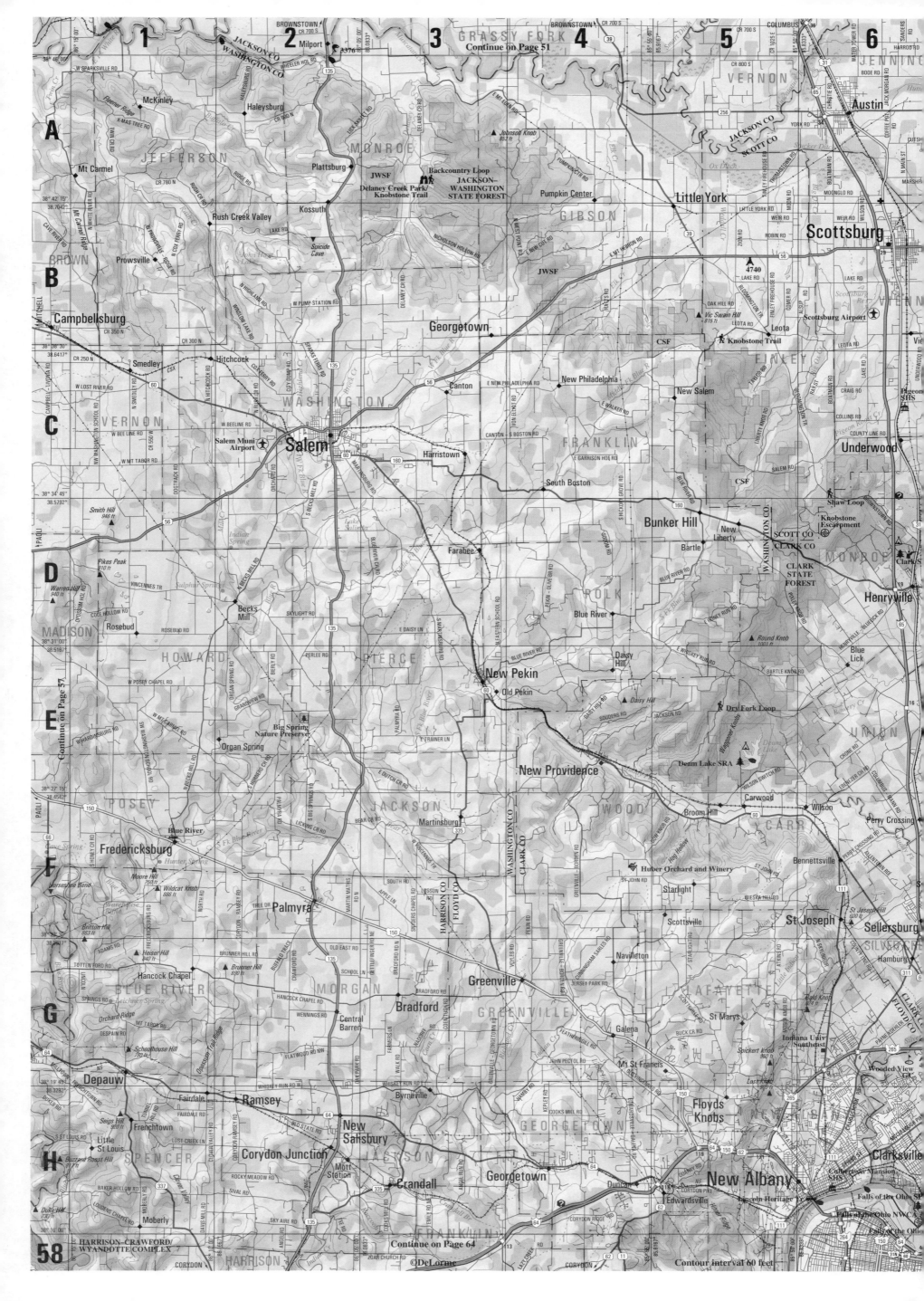

Continue on Page 51

Continue on Page 57

Continue on Page 64

58

HARRISON-CRAWFORD/
WYANDOTTE COMPLEX

©DeLorme

Contour interval 60 feet

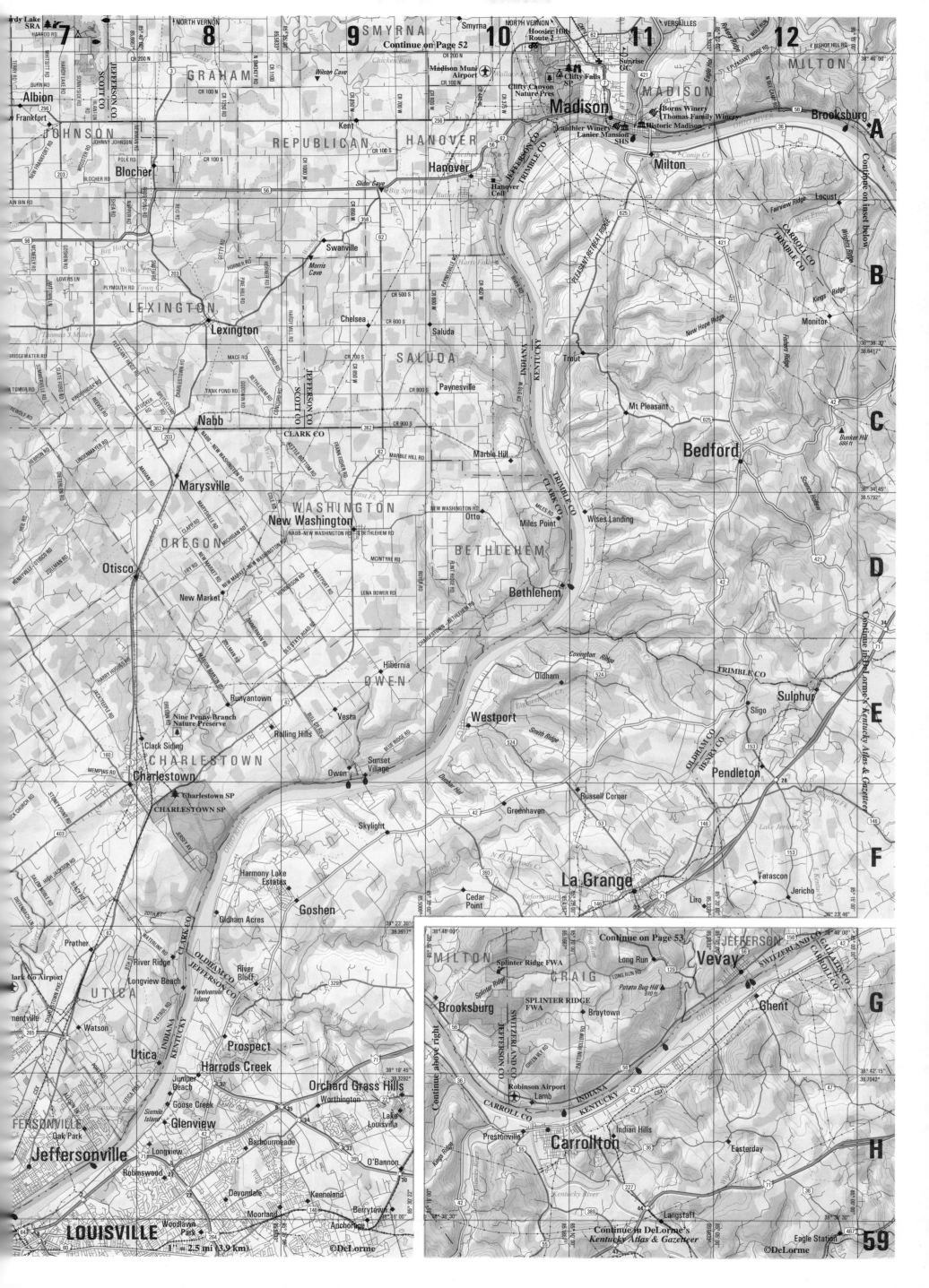

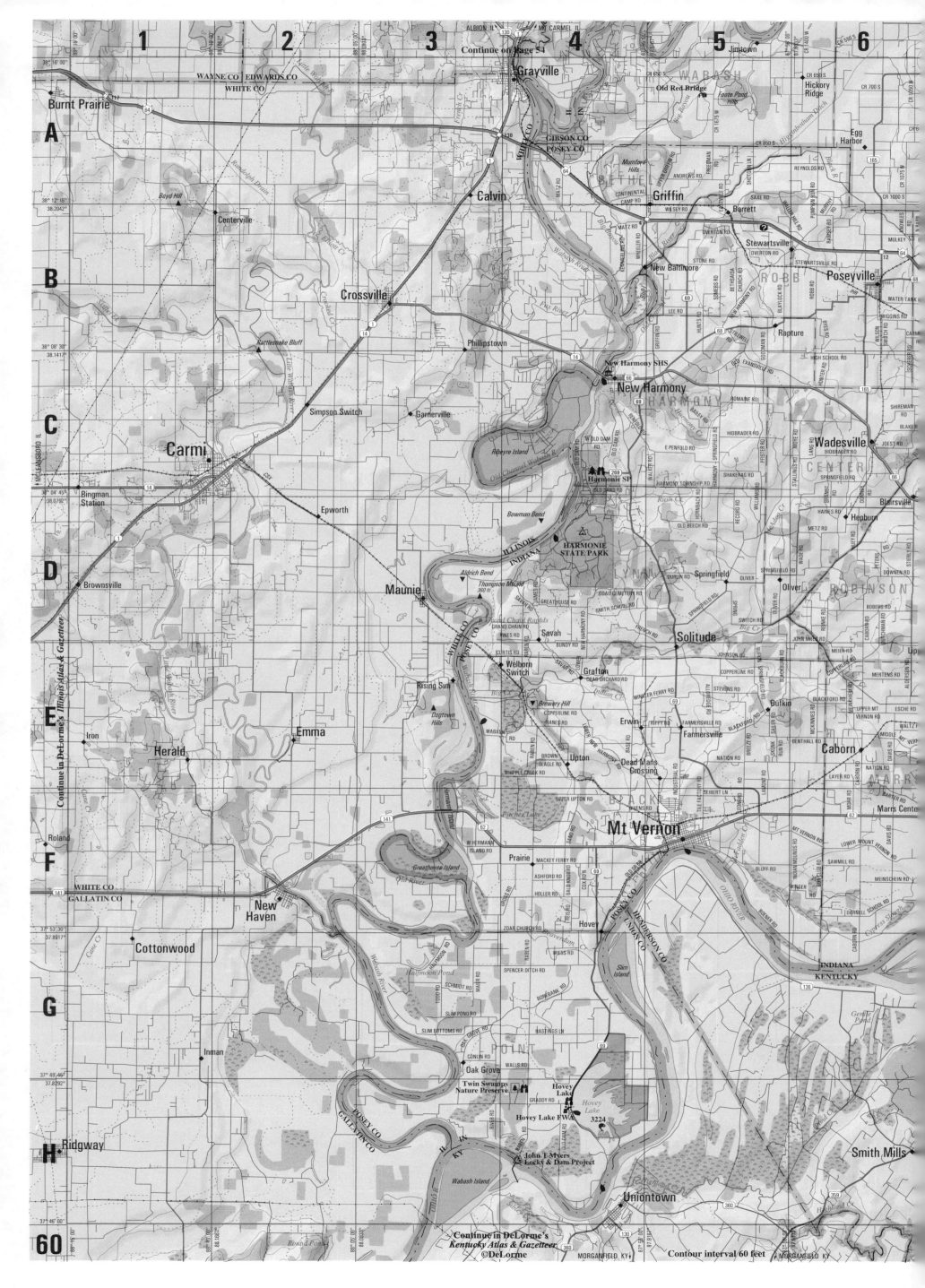

Continue on Page 55

Continue on Page 62

Continue in DeLorme's
Kentucky Atlas & Gazetteer
©DeLorme

1" = 2.5 mi (3.9 km)

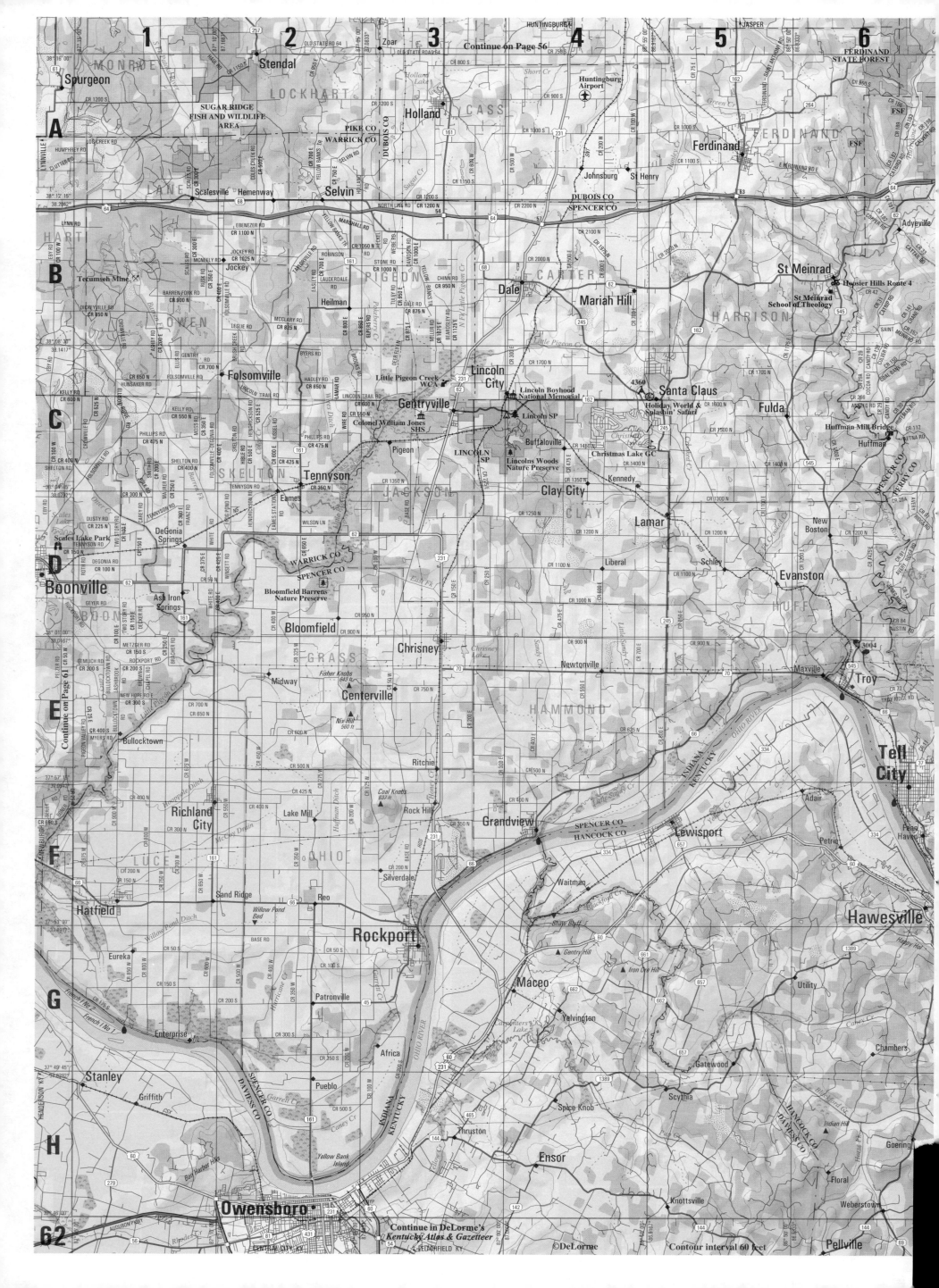

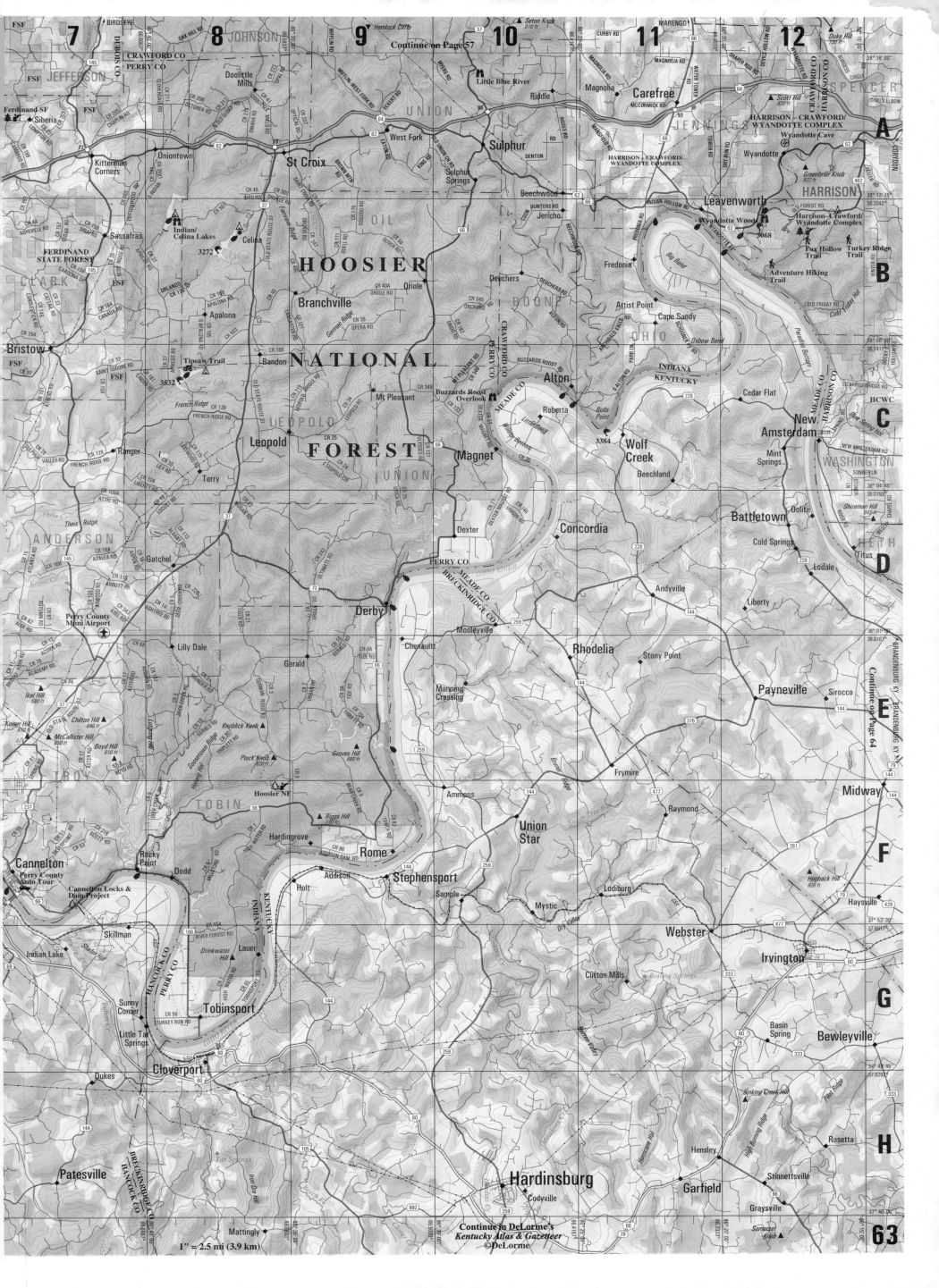

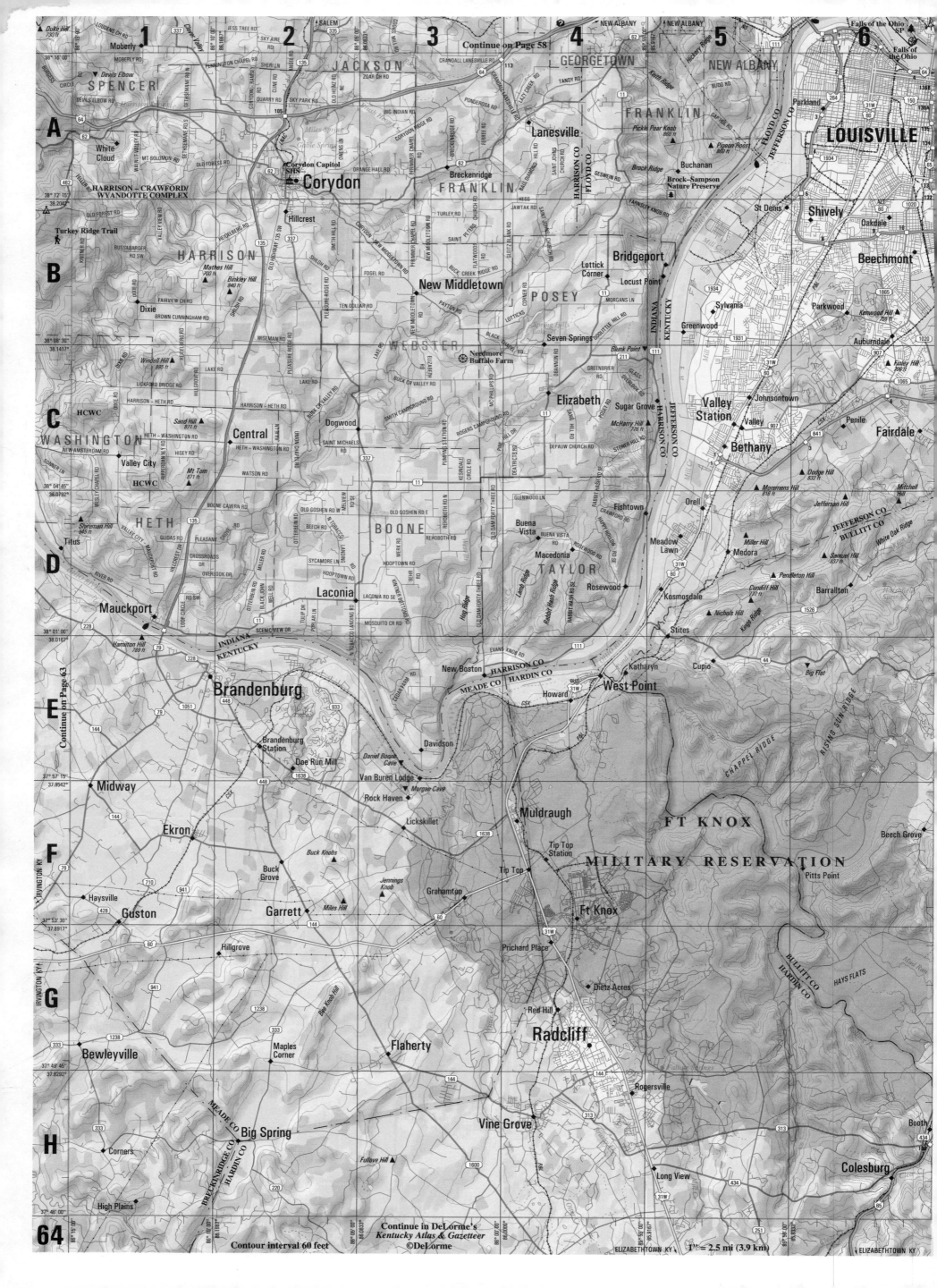